D1565001

SURVIVING
THE STREETS

GIRLS LIVING ON THEIR OWN

RACHEL PFEFFER

GARLAND PUBLISHING, INC.
NEW YORK & LONDON / 1997
CENTER FOR YOUNG WOMEN'S DEVELOPMENT
SAN FRANCISCO / 1997

CHILDREN OF POVERTY

Studies on the Effects of Single Parenthood, the Feminization of Poverty, and Homelessness

edited by

STUART BRUCHEY
University of Maine

A GARLAND SERIES

Library of Congress Cataloging-in-Publication Data

Pfeffer, Rachel.
    Surviving the streets : girls living on their own / Rachel
Pfeffer.
        p.   cm. — (Children of poverty)
    Includes bibliographical references and index.
    ISBN 0-8153-2617-3 (alk. paper)
    1. Street youth—California—San Francisco. 2. Homeless
youth—California—San Francisco. 3. Homeless women—California—San Francisco. 4. Young women—California—San Francisco—Social conditions. 5. Punk culture—California—San
Francisco. I. Title. II. Series.
HV1437.S35P45 1997
362.7'08'6942—dc20   96-46547

Printed on acid-free, 250-year-life paper
Manufactured in the United States of America

Dedicated to
my grandfather, William Pfeffer
and
Maxine Wolfe, Ph.D.

Contents

Preface

While the study is predominantly about white Punk identified young women, we have used this study to create a non-profit organization for young women living on their own of all racial, ethnic, and sexual identities. Street Survival Project, a project of the Center for Young Women's Development, began three years ago upon completion of the study. At any given time, twelve young women under 19 years old are providing survival information to young women on the streets of San Francisco. We have reached over 5,000 young women working in the street economies of San Francisco, employed and trained over 40 young women, promoted staff to management, and held over 600 hours of staff development training. We pay $9.00 per hour and include stress prevention in our benefits package (how Californian). Our work is very stressful. We have a board of directors where 57% are young women under 22 years old. Everyone is involved in the development of ideas and finding the funds to make the ideas a reality. We are selling this book for $40.00 to raise money for new projects. You can also purchase an award winning 5-minute video and obtain lots of free propaganda, so write to us.

This book is a guide to building alliances with young women. We work with a community of young women of all races, mostly poor, homeless or near homeless, drug users, HIV infected and affected young women, girls from immigrant cultures, those who are out lesbians, bisexuals, and straight. We are building a community based on the ideas of this book. We are professional allies, sisters in a new society, members of a village where difficult life experiences are an asset. We have created a place where young women are honored, a place to teach and learn and live well.

By the time you read this book, I will no longer be the Executive Director. It was always the vision that a young woman would be the Executive Director of Street Survival Project. Through an internship process we trained a young woman to take over the leadership. I can however be reached at the address below. I welcome any comments.

Rachel Pfeffer
CFYWD
1095 Market Street, #608
SF CA 94103

CFYWD @igc.apc.org

Acknowledgments

There are many people who have assisted me in different aspects of my life, who have nurtured, challenged and stimulated me. Everyone has tolerated my ranting and encouraged my intellectual development, I love you all. In particular, Maxine Wolfe my advisor, friend and comrade has consistently believed in my ideas, cared about my well being and success and fought for my place in academia. I thank Judith Kubran who hugged me over the phone, listened to me and always had an open heart which was the key for this working class-girl to finish her Ph.D. I thank Leanne Rivlin for her historical place as an intellectual, her huge heart and sharp sensibility. Thank you, Lena Sorensen who has never hesitated to say yes, exchange ideas for hours. Cindi Katz and Michelle Fine, thank you for your time and dedication as members of my dissertation committee. Thank you to my friends who are my family only better - I love you: Richard Weiner, Cynthia Madansky, the artist who also designs beautiful and politically provocative posters, book covers, movies. George Clark, thank you for initiating harm reduction theory education in San Francisco. Bebe Greenberg, thank you for being my sister, my friend, and for sharing all you have with me. Andrea Doremus, thank you for being very old and wise and for loving me. I am also indebted to the encouragement I received from the following courageous and ingenious women: Kelly O'Neill, my work partner extraordinaire, Erica Berman, Lynn Gordon, Jeanne Adelman, Beverly Maher, Kristen Bachler, Chandra Andrews, Lateefah Simon, Nelly Velasco, Danial Dunlap, Nhu Duong, Chris Ebon, Monica Lee, Patricia Lee, Virginia Harris, Carol Leigh, Arlene Stein, Nancy Solomon, Edith Springer, Simmi Gandhi, Emily Newfield, Catherine Teare, Suzanne Rotondo, Christina Gomez, Sara Kershnar,

Alisa Lebow, Lexi Leban, Carol Draizen, Jacque McCright, Tracy Abernathy, Joyce Miller, Terry Greenblatt, Randi Gerson, Lester Olmstead-Rose (not a woman), Donna Saffioti, Marlene Sanchez, Monique Ontiveros, Valentina Rose Austin, Lily Carson, Adriana San Pedro, Stephanie Dunlap, Antigone Hodgins, Ara Wilson and Amy Vickers. My life partner Annie Kastor, who kept me on track, challenged my thinking and appreciated late-night food adventures. Thank you for editing, for listening to me, for working with me, for teaching me new stuff and all the other things I can't really say in public. I love you madly. Preparation for this study was supported by a grant from the Society for the Study of Social Problems, and Gail who helped me financially when I needed it the most.

Surviving the Streets

I

Introduction

"The starting-point of critical elaboration is the consciousness of what one really is, and is 'knowing thyself' as a product of the historical process to date, which has deposited in you an infinity of traces, without leaving an inventory, therefore it is imperative at the outset to compile such an inventory."*

This study was initially an investigation of the spaces used and created by young women who are supposedly "homeless" and "runaway." By interviewing ten young Punk- identified women in San Francisco, and by involving them in a photography project, I intended to insert their voices and experiences into social science research literature. I did not intend to change their lives, re-unite them with their biological "families", measure their mental illness, their self-esteem or pathologize them in any way. I did not intend to morally judge them either. I wanted to document their lives as they would reveal themselves to me, to provide a forum for their voices and develop new theories as they emerged. My methodology was quasi-ethnographic, but with room for responding to situations as they arose. I employed a modified grounded theory approach taking into consideration the institutional consequences of race, class, age, gender-identity, and sexual orientation.

During the course of this study, my focus shifted, as I painfully struggled to identify the borders of resistance, the distance between us as we talked. As I came to "know" the girls, and learned about myself, I identified dominant social doctrines that impacted on my day-to-day work. I began to see these doctrines as borders too. They were clues to my ever-changing, and at the same time static, location as an adult white educated working-class lesbian conducting this research. One would think, (especially from a feminist perspective) that an adult woman, would easily connect with young women/ girls from similar class and race backgrounds. However, the invisible borders I hit up against, again and again, those which made my research so difficult, were all clues to the textuality and power of the historical social science doctrines which have demonized young women on their own. Though I rejected these doctrines, my social/political place and my historical and institutional location was the first thing the young women responded to. I represented the authority of institutions whom young women on-their-own rejected. Constantly unraveling and addressing the layers of borders between us was a painful and important part of conducting this research. The borders changed from day-to-day and they grew and diminished depending on a variety of factors.

Few youth studies in the literature addressed this limitation in epistemology and methodology[1]. The borders which exist between girls and adult women are typically ignored by researchers, or viewed as a dynamic only between their parents, teachers or friends. Thus, researchers claim special non-adult status, because they are "objective" scientists, gathering information in a neutral and responsible way. As a result of this narrow interpretation, young women are epistemologically betrayed. The implications of epistemological betrayal is dangerous to young women and has threatened their survival. The involvement of adult women, historically, in the development of institutions which control young girls on-their-own, based on ideas of gender-morality and demonizing representations, are well known among young women through the day-to-day interactions with adults and their institutions. While individual historical facts may not have been formally known by the young women I met, they knew that I represented a group of people who have participated in their imprisonment and taken away their rights throughout history. Now I claimed to be doing something different, wanting to be "truthful" about their experiences, acknowledging the pain and betrayal in their relationships with adults, and women in particular. Why should they believe or trust me? Throughout this study, I searched for the map to the borders that surrounded us, a way to make these walls visible, so I could see the texture, the history, and the severity of the damage done. The map can locate both physical and ideological sites. Clues to the map are found historically in social science research urban development, labor policies, criminal laws, in the media and in all adult youth interactions, if you look for it.

The young women who participated in this study were living within youth subcultures without adults, experiencing day-to-day hardships, due in large part to moralistic ideology about girls supported by studies completed in a variety of fields. Punk subculture has a history and ideology. There are different factions within the Punk community, which embrace different cultural histories, styles, music and may have different social and environmental experiences. A comparison of different types of Punks is not part of this study because although the participants identified as one type of Punk group, they did not indicate the importance of this distinction. Crossing the invisible borders to meet with them, to go where adult women rarely go, without the intention of saving, incarcerating, or controlling these young women was unusual to them. Proving that I was respectful and consistent was difficult as our relationships were embedded in a complicated personal, social, political history. Sometimes I didn't like them, and sometimes, I suppose, they didn't like me. How we arrived a t those feelings and what they implied, had relatively small consequences on a personal level yet large structural implications at the same time.

In Chapter two, 100 years of interdisciplinary research expose the narrow and static view of girls/young women on their own. Though certain fields of study have exposed information and experiences about women that has changed general knowledge, no field has addressed young women. In fact, our lack of knowledge and distance from them as a group during these last 100 years has created an accumulated hostility and tension. In Chapters three and four, the young women interviews and photographs are testimony to the complex relationships between the young women's environments and social relationships within the context of their youth culture. Initially I asked for demographic information: when they left home, and what the circumstances were that surrounded their leaving. They provided a chronological and rich description of the social and physical environments.

All of the young women had been on their own for two to four years. Their average age was 16. Half of them were from the Bay Area. Two were from Utah, and the remaining were from the east coast and the eastern part of California. Eight of the young women identified as white, one was Jewish, two were mixed-race: African American, Latino and Native American. All of them identified as Punk and straight (heterosexual) though several had sexual relationships with women. The large number of different activities, situations, and environments experienced during the course of one year for most girls on-their-own defies any previous social construction and brings into question the integrity of previous research studies.

I gave all the young women cameras to document their living spaces. The pictures have been stored for safe keeping. No one will ever see them. In the end, using cameras as a research method to capture their seen world was an unethical intrusion, filled with voyeuristic intentions. What became important was how the cameras affected the borders between us and gave me new ways of seeing the young women. The exchange of cameras for their "homeless" experiences, a commodity system which they could easily negotiate and exploit for their benefit, was more interesting than the burden of representing themselves. Yet, I was able to find eight themes among the 40 pictures and to link the description of their environmental experiences to a photograph. I worked backwards, combing through the interviews to find detailed environmental descriptions, and then looked at the photographs to see if there was any representation. Experiences or places which were repeated often in the interviews but were missing from the photos were equally important to the development of the eight themes.

In Chapter five, the connection between newspaper rhetoric and epistemology is discussed. In reviewing the last ten years of articles in five national newspapers about young people on their own, I found more clues to the borders between us. I investigated the social constructions, content analyzed the number and types of representations, the rhetoric, and typifications about young girls on-their-own, created by the newspaper industry in the context of social movements and the evolution of rhetoric about crime, science, family values, the women's movement, and the missing children's movement. I connected this information to the voices and experiences of the young women in this study. In other words, I discovered new borders between us by putting clues together and asking the question: Which institutions benefited from the production of moralistically-based knowledge, images and discourses about young women on their own?

Chapter six provides instructions for crossing invisible borders, ethical considerations when working with young women. Chapter seven is the theory section, and I have approached it by addressing the border between fiction and social science. Eight theoretical issues emerged as a result of my study: 1) there are a variety of youth sub-cultures which girls belong to; 2) the treatment of young women is based on moral codes which are narrow and ideologically flawed; 3) buildings and places have mythology which are important information to young women; 4) homelessness is a social construction; 5)photography as a method for creating representation of girls-on-their-own is flawed; 6) researchers, even if they are women, are not part of the girls' culture and are in fact, viewed by girls as guilty of betrayal until proven innocent; 7) the borders which I have attempted to map are the beginning of a new epistemological landscape and, 8) young women are really smart and talented. I examine these findings in a fictional narrative about Darlene and Lulu, two of the young women I interviewed. Darlene and Lulu, who are older now, reminisce about their girlhood during the late 20th century. The story takes place in the year 2030. I only hope the young women I know make it there.

Notes

* Gramsci in Said, Edward. (1978). *Orientalism*. London: Penguin Books. p. 25

[1] with exceptions, Cain, Maureen. (eds) (1989). *Growing Up Good: Policing the Behavior of Girls in Europe*. Newbury, CA: Sage; Fine, Michelle. (1992).*Disruptive Voices : The Possibilities of Feminist Research*. Michigan: University of Michigan Press.; Lees, Sue. (1993). *Sugar and Spice: Sexuality and Adolescent Girls*. London: Penguin Books; Gilligan , C., McLean Taylor, J., Sullivan, A., (1995) *Between Voice and Silence, Women and Girls, Race and Relationship*. Cambridge, MA.: Harvard University Press.

II

Literature Review

Writings about adolescence span many disciplines. Initially I reviewed only the literature about runaway youth and homeless youth. During the course of the study, and the unraveling of overlapping contexts, I found that the social science literature did not provide a useful or respectful framework to approach my research participants. The literature was in part responsible for creating borders between myself and the young women. I needed to know how extensive the borders were and if fields of research exist that support young women on-their-own, or at least present a more complex understanding of their lives. This directed me to read broadly, incorporating the literature in all the fields which addressed "deviant" or "problematic" young women as a population of study.

The young women who participated in this study were living without adults in youth "subcultures," experiencing day-to-day hardships. I concluded that, in large part, their situations were due to moralistic ideology about girls, supported in a variety of research fields. Crossing the invisible borders in order to meet with these young women was unusual because adults generally approach with the intention of saving, incarcerating or controlling them. Proving that I was respectful and consistent became the main focus of my work. While I understood the personal grounds (with other adults) which mediated their experience of me, I needed to understand the theoretical and methodological history which made our interactions so difficult.

The literature on "deviant" adolescent girls emerges across fields of study with a slightly different understanding of "the problem." Every field investigates girls within the confines of its theories and appropriate methodology, yet reaches conclusions, findings and critical factors which are remarkably similar.* Using methods grounded in logical positivism, social science developed and repeatedly validated the gender correct behaviors which could be viewed in each field. Using biological and psychological theories about girls' "acting-out behaviors", girls—the good and bad—could be coded into predictable and generalized independent variables. These factors or variables are the basis for behavioral theories and conclusions which explain all or part of an individual female personality. Social sciences incorporated environmental co-factors as behavioral determinants and developed theories related almost exclusively to a girl's family and also focused on individual characteristics. Regardless of the field, these individual and family characteristics (including the narrowly defined environmental contexts), are viewed as the causal determinants for "the problems" facing young women and society. The implications of such findings led to laws which restrict and deny civil rights to young people under 18 years old. The laws are carried out unequally among males and females who come in contact with the state and criminal justice systems. Social policies promote female containment to the home and school and the justification for institutional mandates imposed by the state on young women. In essence, young women are political prisoners of North American adults, their "crime" and their "incarceration" rationalized by supposedly objective empirical research.

Environmental psychology offers alternative theories for understanding adolescent development based on ideas of place identity, user activities, privacy, home and territoriality[1]. Radical researchers who redefine and challenge the deterministic and limited behaviors allowed for young women, are generally ignored by mainstream policy makers. Problematizing the environmental context which youth find themselves does not re-frame research objectives and policy interventions for many youth. It does however, provide both the inspiration and critical perspective needed to understand the power dynamics between researchers and young people and how social scientists' ideas of the "deviant" girl is self-serving.

Elevating anything to a "problem" is a competitive process among other would-be problems.[2] The motivations for defining and resolving the problems include: the cultural currency of the problem, the fields' abilities to garner prestige, "expertness", and power and respect for field related theories. Researchers benefit through contract grants, publications and citations and influence the press, service providers and policy makers. Subsequently, few research studies to date have challenged the existing problem domain of girls-on-their-own. It is evident from the literature, that few (if any) of the young women would actually benefit either from the research findings or the process of conducting the research. Since no field is without its politics, the context for creating a "literature" within a field is a critical factor to consider.

In order to create a context and a comparison of emerging historical, economic, psychological and political perspectives, and the policies and institutions which shape our knowledge of "deviant" female adolescents, I reviewed literature on the following topics: 1) child labor history; 2) gender in space, homelessness and urban development history ; 3) delinquency, gangs, runaways, youth prostitution and youth subculture; 4) social science and at-risk youth.

Almost all of the literature about adolescence is based on information about boys. Boys have cultural currency among every sector of our society. Studying boys or the sex-trait differences between boys and girls is not a matter of convenience, but a matter of political, economic and moral urgency dictated by dominant secular and religious ideology. However, it cannot be assumed that if previous studies included girls we would have the information or the context to understand the experiences of girls. Girls exist separate from boys. This seems an obvious point to make, but the underlying assumptions of all the literature comparing boys to girls is that girls exist in a "co-man" environment.[3] The little written about girls-on-their-own does not take into consideration the underlying moral motives to control girls' behaviors. Yet, the underlying motives are directly related to the production of cultural knowledge and attitudes exhibited in all fields of research about girls.

Society in general believes that girls who are without men or family must be policed and followed, whereas un-womaned boys are "independent". This is supported in the literature by myths and imagery that frame girls' singular existence as "at-risk" or "deviant." If we are to accept the girl as un-manned, on a path of economic independence, we should study girls separately. This study, therefore, does not attempt to make a comparison of girls to boys.

Lees discusses how the "double standard of sexual morality and the concern that girls expressed about their sexual reputations were socially structured."[4] Social imbalances for girls are found not only in gender, class and race but in their sexual desires. Girls are steered into particular types of legitimate expression of sexuality, often to the detriment of freedom, and bear the socially-implied moral responsibility of their actions. The implications of incorporating gender broadens the literature review framework to include writings about straight, lesbian, bisexual and questioning female youth. This layer of social relations and experience is one of the most important for young women who must often hide their sexuality from adults and in some cases other youth. It may determine the "subcultures" they affiliate with, or the "street family" they develop, the places they go and the way they survive. In the present study lesbianism or bisexuality will not be treated as a deviant lifestyle or a psychological disorder. Rather, sexuality will be woven into the context in which young lesbians and bisexual young women create their environments.

I begin with a social history of child labor movements, laws and policies and how the underlying premises impact on girls on-their-own, including the development of current problem domains about girls. The changing economic situations throughout the century barely altered the way immigrant poor un-manned women and girls were and are treated in dominant sociological, psychological, underclass, labor, economic, criminological and cultural studies literature. White feminist writers promote a more positive, women-centered context for understanding the impact of gender on labor and macroeconomic changes. Unfortunately, very few white feminist studies include women and girls of color in their studies, an important critical perspective to the connection between economic, sexual and racial exploitation.

GIRL LABOR

The concept of the teenage life course is a cultural product that began with the invention of the adolescent in the second half of the 17th century.[5] During this time period, society moved from a non-capitalist to a capitalist labor system. Labor practices shifted from family, plantation, Hacienda (in Mexico) and Tribal systems to a system where the one-male-European owner employed workers with wages.[6] For indentured servants, slaves and contract laborers, a wage system improved conditions but restricted youth workers.

In the 1600's African children were brought on slave ships, and forced to work for owners.[7] Poor white children were also gathered up by the hundreds from the streets of England and brought to America to work. As the colonies grew in the 1700's, children as young as four-years-old worked as laborers or panhandled.[8] The children were often described as criminals or orphans. Fourteen year old boys were skilled labor apprentices. Girls worked predominantly as domestic workers in poorer conditions and for less pay. Organized labor had no presence in such workplaces.[9]

The rhetoric of concern for children initiated in the 19th century transformed the labor laws of the 20th century, thereby protecting children from the full rigors of adult life and mandating school attendance.[10] Until then, children of poor families and working class families were always part of the work force and nobody bothered to notice or care if children missed their childhood. In 1836, in Massachusetts, the major textile manufacturing center passed laws requiring children under 15 to attend school for 3 months a year. By mandating school attendance, "... in 1850, the important industrial and commercial states reversed the historical predominance of the family as the basis of the laboring class...".[11] Child labor began competing with school.

Rhetoric based on the dangers and evils of the city streets promoted school attendance. From the beginning, school and learning objectives focused on keeping young people out of trouble. In addition, it was critical for schools to provide the new industrialists with socialized white male workers who could handle the new machinery. Most importantly, school was to "...engender respect for authority, self-control, self-discipline, self-reliance and self-respect.".[12] Proponents of expanding the schools campaigned against unattended youth: "If youth were left unattended in the jungles of cities and town, child and youth were likely to fall prey to prostitutes and swindlers and become disruptive to the system...". [13] Fear of cities became endemic in our culture, embedded in ideas of morality. The vocational education movement joined forces with the capitalists to keep children in school. Their recommendations colluded with the industrialist desires; youth should be trained to become obedient laborers. At the same time, school was seen as a diversion program for unfortunate victims of society who would otherwise become criminals.

Academic tracking inculcated the female child's position in the family and the labor hierarchy. In addition, girls were trained for the type of jobs that would be available for her upon completion of her education. This training was reinforced by discipline. The assertion of allegiances to friends was not permitted during class-time and expression of thoughts or feelings were only allowed at certain times. For girls and immigrants, who only sporadically attended school due to family obligations, these rules left them with little social exposure outside of their families and immediate cultural group.

"In 1900, 61% of single European immigrant women over the age of 10 were gainfully employed, compared to only 22% of single white women with U.S. born parents."[14] Immigrant girls and women worked out of necessity. At the same time unpaid domestic work of women and girls was critical to the survival of poor families. In 1910, two-thirds of rural African Americans continued to depend on white landowners for poorly paid work.

Post-abolition work relationships changed for women and girls. One of the ways African Americans put economic pressure on plantation owners was to withdraw women and children from the labor force. This served to create a labor shortage and reduced economic and sexual exploitation by whites of African American women and girls. Their labor at home, preparing food and clothing, was critical to the family's survival and at the same time, gave the family some bargaining power. [15]

Prior to World War II, during a period of domestic unrest, employers began replacing young workers with adults. Adults could handle the new machinery and technology and the new immigrants (particularly Irish women) were better workers for the same wages paid children. Dangerous work environment became the main focus of child labor laws. While many work places were dangerous, this was also a trope or false argument allowing industrialists to appear humane. Child labor laws were supported by capitalists for their own financial interests, not because they were suddenly concerned for the welfare of children. The ideology of the child reformers was, consciously or not, motivated in part by the expansion of the capitalist class. Organized labor adopted the child protection ideology and assisted the capitalist in removing children from the factories. The pretense of protection was part of the rationale for creating the adolescent and carried forward in child serving/saving policies of the late 20th century.

Present day child labor laws prevent young women from employment without the consent of their parent or guardian up to the age of 18. Subsequently, economic resources for young women are severely limited. Economic survival is relegated to illegal earning in exploitative and dangerous environments. Researching among poor young women who desperately need money and have no place to earn beyond the underground economy including selling illegal drugs, prostitution, survival sex and panhandling constructs a border between adults and young women (and researcher and participant). The border is infused with tension and resentment, keeping us apart. While this border is not unique, (in that all poor research participants deal with the inequity), the long history of precluding young women from the labor force creates a resentment among young women on-their-own towards most adults. The young women expected to be paid for their participation in my study, partially because it was common research practice in San Francisco and partially because they needed money. The larger problem of employment was viewed and addressed in a variety of ways among participants.   For the most part, they were proud of their ability to work in the illegal economy. Others tried to work legally but due to the lack of affordable housing, found it impossible to keep a job and spend the time it takes to maintain illegal housing.

THE DEVELOPMENT OF GENDERED PLACES

From the 12th to 19th Century a European slave trade existed for girls and menless women. Menless women include those who were deserted, widowed and lesbians.[16] Poor and homeless women were treated as less then human, and throughout the ages were forced to live in leper colonies, ghettos, and red-light districts. The conceptual paradox of nature and urbanism is analogous to the gender division in society. Women equated with the earth, are transgressive and out of their element when they are in cities; thereby constructing disorder in the universe.[17] The production of urban and suburban environments is linked to concepts of female danger and desire and other socially motivated moral ends.

Architects and planners of social space control these dangers by controlling women and girls. Normative behaviors are institutionalized through ethical codes, family values, religious systems and imagery,   urban landscapes, public/private spaces and the collective cultural meaning of home. The imposition of these normative behaviors serve to quell the fears among "society". The home is associated with properness, good health, gender appropriateness, and family values by urban and youth policy makers. As a result, housing and public environments are not produced for young women who live on their own.

Society's preoccupation with the family home, its social prestige, and the concept of self-expression through decoration, is the basis of urban land development policies. These policies promote social homogeneity, intolerance of different peoples and a false sense of family self-sufficiency. They also promote the limited role of women in society, slavery, racism, class segregation and institutionalized consumerism.[18] The home, and the setting for the home, become linked to such ideas as civic responsibility, good family values and like-mindedness, as represented in the repetitious pattern of house design for middle and working class families. Poor people have a different form of repressive housing in which amenities are absent and disease is rampant. In the early years of the republic, national housing types were promoted by builders to produce a good "American" family. Even housing for slaves was premised on the white owners' ideas of an "American" family with slaves. Owners believed that slave cabins would stabilize plantation society. In reality, the intent of slave cabins was to maintain control and promote racist ideas of sexuality, family, black personality traits, cleanliness and the differences that justified segregation.

Worker housing, created in the late 18th century by textile mill owners, provided small spaces for many workers to reside in. Children would play outside until they were old enough to work in the mills. At this time, many of the workers were white European-born and English speaking yet were viewed as poor, lazy and potential criminals. The mill owner was publicly congratulated (similarly to slave owners) for providing the religious training and work ethic needed to create good "American" families. Experimental boarding housing for young rural girls coming to the textile towns provided moral and cultural education that the middle class could endorse and factory owners were again applauded for their social innovation. Eventually, however, the women organized and the myths of mill town virtues were dispelled through the publication of a workers' magazine. The conditions deteriorated as the influx of immigrants created increased crowding and factory owners became less concerned with their image. Modernization changed the industrialists' priority from a good worker environment to a good "American" product.

The concept of linking an individuals' character to the home shifted from industry to different institutional and professional domains. Educational philosophers, architects and landscapers debated and produced the policies and residential designs that would promote the family values already established as "American" values. Narrowly conceived concepts became connected to the correct behaviors of young women and the family and were incorporated into the discourse of design and home. In the late 1800's, designs connected to nature were viewed as morally appropriate for perpetuating a sound and good family. Well-ordered natural systems (i.e., bigger windows) were the basis for developing a physical connection between the home and the outdoors. [19]

The goal for developing middle class suburbs in the late 19th century was safe and secluded environments, far from the dangerous city. It was generally accepted among architects, landscapers, planners, and scientists that city streets were unnatural environments, unfit for children. The growth of suburban developments promoted a suburbanite culture. The current practice of sending young "delinquent" women to closed institutions for their "own good" is in part based on these early ideas of a good environment for a good girl. Most of the participants in this study had been institutionalized, removed from their support networks and friends. In most situations, the young women ran from these places, re-uniting themselves with their "street families".

In the early 20th century cities, reformers were critical of the conditions for poor tenement dwellers. Guided by the same ideology as the suburban promoters, reformers wanted to control family behaviors and address the lack of moral character found in tenement families, among women in particular. Deterministic design solutions to this "American" problem included the development of back alleys to keep children and women off the main streets. "Privacy was the cornerstone for promoting individual baths and rooms, instilling in the young the value of individual property rights and sexual morality." [20] In 1902, Sociology Professor Charles R. Henderson at the University of Chicago warned: "A communistic habitation (that is, a tenement house) forces the members of a family to conform to insensible communistic modes of thought."[21] Privacy and sexual morality were encoded into laws against prostitutes who rented the first floors of tenements (at higher rates). The purpose of the law was to discourage prostitutes from bringing customers where children would see them.

The management of prostitution and urban policy share conceptions of deviance and control both in rhetoric and in a structural context. As the 20th century progressed, civil rights movements and grass-roots organizing influenced design and urban policy. Women became part of a more ambiguous rhetoric, but young girls remained in the rhetoric of previous centuries.

Part of the history of homeless/runaway girls involves measures taken by society to deal with women, girls and poor people in general. The relationship between space, power and gender was never made explicit in spatial production policies or design guidelines yet the reciprocity between space and status was a constant re-negotiation and re-creation of the existing stratification system. Poor people, women and girls of color have never had full rights in the city. Yet, industrialization pulls them there, providing little support against the stratification system. In fact, there are very few dominant social environments where these populations have and feel a sense of belonging and community acceptance. This factor continues to be one of the major struggles for girls on-their-own.

SOCIAL SCIENCE AND BAD GIRLS

In the early 20th century, Hall made influential conceptual links as he developed the first physical and developmental stage theory of children, based on the paradigm of natural order.[22] The paradigm did not change dominant society's treatment of youth. It reinforced negative and disrespectful views and continues to rationalize current legal policies and services, negatively impacting poor young women on their own. Those youth who did not succeed in the deterministic development outlined by Hall were used by a variety of fields during the next 60 years to develop problem domains. For example, criminologists and sociologists (and later underclass "scholars") studied the cause(s) of youth deviance, known generally as delinquency.[23]

In the 1920's psychologists, educators and psychiatrists addressed adolescence and delinquency and concluded that delinquency was caused by multiple factors, such as the interaction between genetic and environmental factors. Environmental factors were defined as family, school, and peer interactions. "The dominance of psycho-pathological paradigms in welfare professionals' assessment of the needs of adolescent girls has been well used."[24] Psychological research during the early part of the 20th century focused on the pathology of behaviors leading to abnormal female activities defined by the extensive sex-trait stereotype research industry.[25] Running away, becoming a prostitute, becoming involved with drugs or alcohol, having pre-marital sex (with a boy, of course) or becoming a teen parent are behaviors linked to low self-esteem, deviant sex-trait attributes, and a developmental stage of rebelliousness. Social psychology, social work and sociology expands the concepts of individual pathology to the family. In the 1990's, researchers studying runaways found another reason for youth on-their-own. A new term was coined, "throwaways", referring to parental rejection.[26] This rejection was investigated and is related to substance abuse, physical violence and sexual violence perpetrated predominantly by males in the family. Studies found that between 5% to 100% (depending on the type of sample) of runaway or throwaway youth experienced sexual abuse in the family.[27] In spite of this finding, program interventions insist that youth be re-united with families who are then mandated to receive counseling and referrals. Thus, girls belong at home. Youths who come from family environments with no home are removed from the family and placed in the foster care or group home industry. In a few instances, families may receive temporary housing, but few housing solutions exist for poor people and none exist for girls-on-their-own.

Early psychological research studies support theories of runaway girls generally based on the male model of causal variables related to adventure and the search for identity.[28]

Research has since found correlations between running away and family instability, as well as poor living conditions, and problematic adolescent behavior.[29] For girls, distinctive gender-related behaviors are connected to running away including: vagrancy, sexual promiscuity, prostitution, suicide attempts, and pregnancy. [30]Running away, according to sociologists and criminologists, is highly correlated with a future life of adult crime. Females are criminalized for different behaviors than males. For example, engaging in sex is rarely a crime which is criminalized or pathologized for heterosexual men.

The field of psychology also investigates runaways from the focus of motivation, strain and control theories. These theories are used in analytic frameworks in order to construct a taxonomy of runaways. Psychologist developed a systematic formula for determining causal correlations between individual personality traits and family in an effort to predict who would runaway. Homer articulates the dominant social science explanation for girls who leave home for more than 24 hours. Girls fall into two categories: running to (romantic relations, sex, drugs, adventure, stimulation) and running from (conflicts at home, school, rejection). This research is usually cited in order to critique its' shortcomings including small sample size, the static nature of a non-static situation, and lack of psychological personality traits associated with the running to and running from behavior. Additional psychological studies clear-up these methodological and theoretical flaws, but follow-up studies provide few new conclusions and instead focus on treatment recommendations based on personality traits. [31]

This type of research associates the appropriateness of girls' behaviors with gender roles. Connected to this narrow approach is the interpretation of girls' words during interviews by treatment center social workers. For example, when a client was asked why she left and reported "because I felt like it." She is interpreted by the authors as having an internal locus of control, and put her in the category of girls who run to rather than from.[32] The researcher's lack of consideration for the context of the interview and the implications of revealing information, is thoughtless. This problem occurs over and over again in the academic literature and even among feminist researchers who interpret statements by young women to accommodate the ideological basis of psychology.[33] Unacknowledged borders among researchers create more borders. The consequences of this betrayal is the difficult relationship young women have with feminism. Feminist researchers, of the same race and class mis-interpret girls' words for the same reason as other social science researchers; attempting to fit their voices into feminist theories.

Like sociology, criminology and other social sciences, psychology has its own interpretation and typologies for these young women. However, the prevailing focus of "research" is to problematize individual or family behaviors. Psychology is particularly diligent in pursuing research that debases young women. Studies typically investigate sexual and other "deviant" behaviors that may be determinants of running away. Green and Esselsyn, for example, studied girls who ran away from the juvenile justice system.[34] They describe these young women in three categories: 1) rootless: exhibiting a lack of self-discipline, and indulging in pleasure seeking behavior; 2) anxious runaways; those who feel powerless in the face of their personal problems; and 3) terrified runaways: those escaping from alcoholic parents, incest and threats to their lives. Stierlin's mental institution sample based on a typology of runaways, describes two different kinds of runaways. [35] Both exhibit individual and/or family pathology. One type includes a gender differentiated description. This is the "casual runaway," one who seeks pleasure and is "uncontrollable. " This group is generally found among boys, but the female counterpart is the "sweet bad girl, who is characterized by impulsivity, pleasure seeking, sexual promiscuity and hysterical, depressive character structure". The research posits a new and supposedly more thorough taxonomy, including socio-economic status, gender and age. The premise underlying the articulation of two classes and seven types of runaways is the level of separation from parents and school. The first class of runaways is not highly delinquent and predominantly male. The second class is delinquent, alienated and rejected by parents and school. Across socioeconomic lines, girls form the majority of the second class. Teachers label girls as uninspired by education and careers and girls have the highest drop-out rate from school. Girls characterized as angry, rebellious, with a high level of commitment to their friends and a rejection of parents are categorized as highly delinquent.[36]

In an article in the *Journal of Developmental Psychology*, the researchers intended to unravel girls' delinquency from a biological, dispositional and contextual perspective. Girls are reduced to the one biological event -menarche- linked to behavioral changes toward sexuality and misbehavior.[37] "Previous research has shown that early puberty is associated with problems in girls."[38] Researchers study the difference between all-girls schools and the mixed school environment as a possible influence in the personal and social significance of menarche. No other description of the context is offered, yet environment is considered a key element in the experience of girls. It was the hope of the authors that their research would inform parents of girls' behavior problems in early childhood. The research would also influence parents' decisions about school for girls, given that menarche could alter girls' behavior. The authors found that the experience of menarche was more difficult for girls in a mixed gender school and that deviant girls (active, disruptive, sexual) behave more deviant in mixed gender schools. The study concludes that menarche is neutralized in a same sex school and normative controls suppress deviant activities among girls. The research findings perpetuate the notion that girls should be controlled and scientific guidance is offered to parents. This type of research ignores lesbians and bisexual young women, factors which could be important in understanding the concept of behavior "problems" among a sexually diverse group of young women. The absence of lesbian, bisexual or girls questioning their sexual identity in previous studies allows for the misinterpretation of behaviors and actions based on a heterosexual model of proper behavior. These continual misintepretations create more borders between my participants and myself.

During the 20th century, sociologists focused on the criminal "problems" created by deviants who threatened good

"American" society.[39] One of the sociologists' jobs was to develop objective knowledge about the characteristics of people who commit crimes. Using explanatory categories such as age, ethnicity, parental background, social class, employment status and school attendance, researchers found evidence that delinquency is evident only in a specific stratum of society and almost without exception among males. Attempts to understand women and girls defined as deviant focussed on their involvement in crime and gangs.[40] Miller emphasized the role of class in his research. He believed that delinquent activity needed to be investigated with reference to the values upheld by girls in the context of their lifestyles. Girls who habitually become involved in violence, and crime must be examined in comparison with their peers who are not deviant. Miller believed that part of societal shock about girls involved in "delinquent" behavior arose from the stereotypical views of middle class white women and children. Generally, the efforts of sociology support negative and de-contextualized perceptions of people of color, poor, working class and underemployed immigrants, gang affiliated members, prostitutes, youth and criminals. It is these stereotypes that lay the groundwork for the social service industry.

More recent sociological studies about gangs and other organized groups of young people offer a better sense of how class, race, violence and exploitation actually operate within the gang.[41] However, when any mention of girls is made, the theoretical male gang member model is used to understand the experiences of girls. Girls are rarely interviewed by the researcher. Class, and leisure time are the factors used in an effort to understand the options available for girls and the mediating variables to their behavior in gangs. Only in studies exclusively about girls in gangs or girl gangs is there a discussion of gender.[42] In these studies sociologists and cultural studies scholars talk to the young women and use frameworks of analysis which in part emerge from their study. The methodology used result in a clearer picture of the experiences of girls, including girls of color and their subcultures. However, none of the studies consider sexuality as a mediating factor influencing experiences and decisions. Studies about girls do not have to focus on only lesbian, bisexual and questioning youth to include sexuality as part of the framework. Many girls are sufficiently closeted even with their closest peers. Researchers may be talking to a lesbian and not even know it. It is important to represent the full range of experiences for girls so that their lives are made known to the general public.

For complex reasons, the cultural currency of studies which challenge dominant ideas about girls is minimal. It is due in part to the traditional research ethos of objectivity, often precluding researchers from working in tandem with community organizations, service providers and policy makers. Also, research that does not support dominant ideas about girls and women is not widely received or considered influential by other researchers. Finally, the mainstream press does not report on non-mainstream findings, leaving the study in the inaccessible format of a book or journal article, most likely known only to university students and researchers.

The implications of the obscurity of important research and research particularly focused on girls' sexuality creates service organizations with little support to combat homophobia. In addition, the criminalization of gays and lesbians infringes on the ability of organizations to reach out to young gay and lesbians.[43] The lack of support within the queer community and general youth serving organizations creates a service gap which the gay and lesbian community only recently began to address. Unfortunately, even within the gay and lesbian community there are class and racial biases which negatively impact on gay and lesbian youth organizations. Generally, poor lesbian and bisexual girls are without support. Another border between myself and the research participants exists as a result of these historical and current responses to queer youth. My location as a lesbian researcher offers little comfort to young lesbian or bisexuals who find themselves outside of the "community" I supposedly represent.

CRIMINALIZING GIRLS

The first large scale and organized imprisonment of
women occurred in the U.S. when many women's
reformatories were established between 1870 and
1900. Women's imprisonment was justified not because
the women posed a public safety risk, but rather
because they were seen to be in need of moral revision
and protection. [44]

Women and young women have always been part of gangs, but
their violent behavior was usually ignored unless it directly
challenged the racist, sexist, homophobic and classist policies
of their day. [45] Historically reform policies were used to justify
incarceration of white working class women who acted outside
of the true nature of womanhood. Women of color and African
American women were always incarcerated in prisons and
treated like the male prisoners. because their occasional
violent behaviors could easily be linked to the challenge of
racism and sexism. [46] The "war on ...." policies of the last 30
years are imbedded in sexist and racist policies of punishment
for "immoral" non-criminal activities.

Girls and women are criminalized for non-criminal
activities such as lesbianism, drug use among pregnant women,
and "crimes" committed due to violent systemic victimization. [47]
The American legal system has a tendency to regulate through
concepts of dichotomous categorization. [48] The legal system
traps young women, lesbians in particular, into categories that
conflict with their experiences. What is legal and right and
what is illegal and immoral seem to be identifiable within the
legal system. But when survival is dependent on breaking into
an abandoned building and having sex with a guy even if you
are a lesbian, the terms become clouded and irrelevant. As a
lesbian, is she moral and right to be having heterosexual sex?
As an un-emancipated minor without shelter, is she a criminal
for breaking and entering? What measures can be used to
understand the experiences of young lesbians on-their-own?

Evaluating the legal system and its applicability to the survival of young lesbians on-their-own is critical to understanding the borders between adults and youth and the services developed or undeveloped. If we accept the terms legal and illegal as set forth by the existing legal system, synonymous with moral and immoral, we limit the options available to young women and our connections to them.

The growth of the criminal justice system during the 20th century was accomplished through a economically rationalized policies. The result was more prisons, the abandonment of any pretense of jail-term rehabilitation, reduction of health care and mental health services for poor people, criminalization of homelessness, and detainment of youth after arrest without bail.

The demonized young woman is African American, or Latina, is poor, violent, and part of a gang. She is described more violently in the press then in actuality. According to a U.S. Public Health Service report, 71% of all female teenage parents have adult partners over age 20. Even though many more births are caused by men over 25, the media only portrays high school boys by their choice of terms and images. The media blames young women while giving adult males a break. The collusion of official reports and media distortions define youth and crime as the same. The lack of content and fairness in studies about youth, and young women in particular, creates borders between adults and youth. The seriousness of creating an environment where youth are feared for the "crimes" they commit, where the two sides of the "story" come only from adults, supports an institutional response focused on mending young people not their environments.

Social inequities are often evident in the environment. Environmental psychologists in the 1970's laid the groundwork for investigating the socio-cultural and physical world in an attempt to understand the relationship between individuals, their identity, and their developmental process.[49] Even still, researchers have not adapted their understanding to include the socio-cultural world of the female adolescent. The youth-at-risk paradigm provides a new currency for old research.

ARE YOUTH AT RISK IN THEIR ENVIRONMENTS?

> A new class of untouchables' is emerging in our inner cities, on the social fringes of suburbia and in some rural areas: young people who are functionally illiterate, disconnected from school, depressed, prone to drug abuse and early criminal activity, and eventually, parents of unplanned and unwanted babies. These are the children who are at high risk of never becoming responsible adults.[50]

The identification of high risk youth is the major buzz word/category for funding and program intervention in the 1990's. Social scientists (generally medical allied professionals, i.e., public health researchers and pediatricians) were the whistle blowers of the late 1980's. They "saw" the increased deterioration of youth despite multiple and varied interventions, "community-based" movements, and governmental support. Ultimately nothing was working to change the behaviors of youth. The major goals of the high risk saviors were to determine who needed help before the problem behavior exhibited and create a sort-of mathematical formula for assessing deviant youth behaviors. The assumptions underlying much of the research of "youth at risk", in particular female adolescents on-their-own, are problematic.

Dominating most research efforts is an image of "safe youth." The stereotypcial "safe youth" promoted and unchallenged by behavioral science fields for 100 years, is white, male, middle class and secure in a home with two parents. Missing from this image is an understanding of how youth on-their-own experience safety and create it in their daily lives. Assumptions about safety provide a justification for policy focused on prevention of "risk," resulting in the study of the social class of youth who are still in homes, rather than youth who are homeless. Further, this approach avoids understanding the economic and physical dangers of homelessness. The dominant research ideology provides a disease model of youth, justifying policies focused on individual treatment. Policies pressure families to adhere to specific behavioral changes rather than promote social systemic changes.[51]

Definition of the problem domain remains stuck in specific characteristics and predisposing factors or determinants of behavior (i.e., social status). The main areas of high risk behavior fall into four problem groups: delinquency, substance abuse, early childbearing and school failure. Based on definitions of high risk, target populations are quantified, first by estimates of prevalence and second by estimates of numbers of risk. The formula used to assess risks is based on insurance actuarial methodology-risk probability. Risks are constituted by the individual academic fields who previously conducted and defined juvenile delinquency research. Then, probabilities are calculated to define the risk. There is no longitudinal research on youth who "display high risk behaviors" and the method used by risk assessors assumes that nothing changes for the youth over time. Finally, the predictors of the specific behaviors are reified in order to identify the characteristics of those who will fall into the risk groups. Behaviors with negative outcomes are included in a psychiatric diagnosis called "conduct disorder."[52] The symptoms of this diagnosis include multiple behaviors extended over a six-month period. The symptoms include: truancy, stealing, cheating, running away, fire-setting, cruelty to animals or persons, unusually early sexual intercourse, substance abuse, breaking-in and entering and excessive fighting. When three or more of these behaviors occur before the age of 15, the child is considered unmanageable or out of control, and can be diagnosed. Recent studies suggest that conduct disorders may lead to delinquent behaviors and that delinquency may lead to criminal careers.[53] Policy makers interested in interventions to prevent youth-at-risk behaviors suggest that service providers utilize behavior disorder categories in diagnosing them. The problem with this method is that the behaviors become reified and subsequently bind social knowledge with inaccurate analyses. The problems do not get ameliorated, youth continue to be misunderstood and are further alienated from adults and the social services offered.   The borders between youth and adults are substantiated by at-risk researchers.

There are few at-risk researchers who offer a phenomenological perspective on risks as assessed by youth.[54] In the 1990's the federal government supported ethnographies of street kids in an attempt to reduce the spread of HIV disease. Irwins' research rejects the actuarial approach to calculating probabilities by asking youth how risky certain behaviors might be over time. Incorporating both the opinions of youth and time into a broader understanding of risk is important. However, the basic categories of risk are codified in the ideology and theories defined by social scientists during the last century. Operationalizing risk offers a new paradigm embedded in new and old cultural currency for professionals researching youth. Asking youth about their explanatory framework for defining risk may be important to addressing borders between adults and youth and then again, risk may be too embedded in an adult framework to have meaning for young women on their own.

Risk calculations are significantly based in the research and theories formulated in the field of psychology.[55] The main underpinning of the field is to differentiate youth from adults and create a gauge of normal and abnormal behavior then utilized by parents and professionals to control and treat children. A youth displaying abnormal behavior is at risk for not growing up to be a responsible adult. According to at-risk theories, adolescents are not yet adults because they have not achieved independence from their families, developed skills for problem solving, awareness of their self-definition or own set of values, and do not have the capability to build the boundaries of a physical home to protect themselves. [56] Yet, each day, homeless girls create both their physical and social worlds.

Particular behaviors which constitute risks for girls are viewed through a lens which recognizes girls' experiences are both unique and linked inextricably to their status as young women. The underlying moralistic assumptions of this concept remain unchallenged in the current youth-at-risk interventions and research.   Policy makers use these developmental assumptions to create interventions for "youth at risk" and define the youth experience in a manner which does not include girls on their own and cannot speak to their reality or needs. We know that in many cases "risk taking behavior" occurs because young people are in powerless and dangerous situations (i.e., adult abuse, unstable housing, poverty, gang culture). Recent studies on the sociology of gangs and street workers highlight what is categorized as risk taking behavior is sometimes the result of choosing the lesser of two dangers for economic and social security.[57] Paradoxically, the concept of youth at risk maintains an image of the young person as both victim and victimizer. [58] Consequently, existing social services range from the therapeutic to the disciplinary. These forms of interventions are intended to treat and prevent further acts which are dangerous to the "well being" of youth as well as mainstream them back into a "safe youth" situation. Most interventions disregard the context for youth actions.

HOMELESS YOUTH

Ruddick's article on the new geography of homelessness explores the theory that homeless youth are attracted to certain areas within a city for different reasons than adults.[59] The premise of a geography of homelessness was first posited in Dear and Wolch's work.[60] Specific urban environments were found to support large concentrations of homeless adults due to the initial development of city ghettos and later because de-institutionalized mentally ill patients could only find inexpensive accommodations in these urban ghettos. The destruction of single room occupancy hotels, the main type of housing available for poor people, disables the fragile social networks created by homeless people.[61] In the 1920's and 30's, according to Ruddick, youth on their own did not mingle with adults who were considered hoboes. The boys (I assume, White) were integrated into menial labor jobs during World War I, such as "newsies." In 1988, after talking to youth in Hollywood, Ruddick found that five areas of concern determine where youth will "spatially filter" including: safety from violence, ability to avoid police authority, the presence of a large stable population of other youth, an accessible underground economy where they can blend in, and participation in "oppositional" subcultures.

Unlike adults, the location of services is not a factor in determining areas where youth are attracted. A study by Brockman found that "...when runaways were taken out of Hollywood to foster homes in other parts of the country they often ran right back again."[62] This may be due to resistance to the child protection system, which most young women find difficult unless the home they are placed in provides a new freedom. For example, young lesbian and bisexual women in my study stayed in their foster placement after they were placed with adult lesbians who supported their sexuality.

In Rivlin's essay on the variety of homeless people not necessarily recognized as such, youth are among the new homeless.[63] Until 1985, the Coalition for the Homeless did not consider youth as part of their constituency. The life experiences of female youth who live on their own are both similar to adult homelessness and unique to their gender, race and legal implications of their age. Our physical experience of them in the streets, our characterization of where they are and the etiology of their existence is typified by the Times Square hustlers, the Lower East Side Squatters, the Haight Ashbury Hippies, the Los Angeles Punks and Gangsters and younger children living with their homeless families. There are no studies to date which focus on young women, investigating the circumstances of their life experiences. However, the youth homelessness of the 1990's, especially among girls, is a complex arrangement negotiated by urban developers, advocates, the street economy, youth subcultures and the moralistic representation and relative invisibility of girls who live on-their-own.

SUMMARY

In this chapter I review the range of work written about girls-on-their-own. Historically, across different fields in academia, girls are mis-categorized and mis-represented because researchers use male models of life experiences and gender-based morality as the framework for their studies. Studies of homelessness, homeless youth, youth at risk, runaways, delinquent youth, gangs, deviance among girls, and prostitution indicate that each field problematizes different aspects of girls, yet concludes and recommends similarly. In addition, each field has benefited over time from grants, contracts and prestige without necessarily being interested in benefiting girls. Rather than challenge and redefine terms based on a grounded knowledge of the population they are studying, researchers accept negative myths and stereotypes. These myths reify this population using information from counselor reporting. Researchers wrongly accept and present research findings based on participant non-participation to describe the experiences of girls. When researchers include girls' reporting, usually one-fifth of the study participants were girls. Researchers extrapolate and generalize from boys' experiences. Their findings support male/female gender-role behaviors and debasing and oppressive conceptual frameworks. These explanatory frameworks presented extensive contradictions to my study. Throughout time, social scientists have not developed new concepts and methods to embrace girls-on-their-own in a positive light.

The historical and current doctrines in social science literature support the subsequent policies that are explicitly negative and negating of young women's experiences. The comprehensive and systematic invisibility of girls, lesbian and bisexual young women in studies about youth and their subcultures hurts the relationships between adult women and young women. The double standard of sexual morality, the inclusion of racism and classism in studies and the dichotomies (good girls, bad girls) in the legal system are serious problems. The survival of young women is at stake. We must analyze the

usefulness of existing theories and policies. We must develop
an understanding of the borders created and canonized in our
disciplines. Narrow and simplistic explanations of young
women's experiences only increases the borders between us and
threatens the subsistence of our younger sisters. Unraveling the
complex relationships between the social production of urban
neighborhoods, the history of property rights and squatter
communities, the spatial context for gender, class,
homelessness, sexual identity, and urban myths reveals the
borders, and the tensions between adults and young women on-
their-own.

Notes

*   Shacklady Smith, L. (1976). "Sexist assumptions and
female delinquency." in Smart & Smart (Eds.), *Women
Sexuality and Social Control.* pp.74-87.
[1]   Alissi, A. (1970). "Delinquent sub-cultures in
neighborhood settings: A social system perspective." *Journal of
Research on Crime and Delinquency, 7(1),* 46-55.; Hart, R.
(1979). *Children's experience of place: A developmental Study.*
Irvington Press.; Lynch, K . (1977.). *Growing up in cities: Studies
of the spatial environment of adolescence.* Cambridge, MA.:
MIT Press.; Newman, P. (1973). "Social settings and their
signficance for adolescent development." *Adolescence,* 11(43),
405-417; Rivlin, L. & Wolfe, M. (1985). *Institutional settings in
children's lives .* New York: John Wiley & Sons.
[2]   Gusfield, J. (1981). *Drinking-driving and the symbolic
order.* Chicago & London: University of Chicago Press.
[3]   Cain, M. (Eds). (1989). *Growing up good: Policing the
behavior of girls in europe.* Newbury, CA: Sage.
[4]   Lees, S., cited in Cain, 1989.p.19
[5]   Musgrove, F. (1964.). *Youth and social order.*
Bloomington, IN.: Indiana University Press.
[6]   Amott, T., & Matthaei, J. (1991). *Race, gender and work*
Boston: South End Press.

7   Zinn, H. (1980). *A People's History of the United States*. New York: Harper and Row Publishers.

8   Smith, P. (1984). *The Shaping of America, A People's History of the Young Republic* Vol. 3. New York: McGraw Hill Book Co.

9   Amott & Matthaei, 1991

10   Aronowitz, S. (1992). *False promises*. Durham and London: Duke University Press.; Best, J. (1990). *Threatened children: Rhetoric and concern about child victims*. Chicago: University of Chicago Press; Rivlin & Wolfe, 1986 .

11   Aronowitz, 1992, p.72

12   Aronowitz, 1992, p.73

13   Aronowitz, 1992, p.73

14   Amott & Matthaei, 1991, p.105

15   Amott & Matthaei, 1991

16   Golden, S. (1992). *The women outside: Meanings and myths of homelessness*. California: University of California Press.

17   Wilson, E. (1991). *The sphinx in the city: urban life, the control of disorder, and women*. Berkeley, CA.: University of California Press.; Hayden, D. (1981). *The grand domestic revolution* . Cambridge: MIT Press.;Wright, G. (1983). *Building the Dream*. Cambridge: MIT Press.

18   Wright, 1981

19   Wright, 1981

20   Wright, 1981, p.126

21   Wright, 1981, p.126

22   Hall, G. S. (1915). *Adolescence*. (Vol. 2), New York: Appelton & Co.

23   Chesney-Lind, M. (1991). "Patriarchy, prisons and jails: A critical look at trends in women's incarceration." Paper presented at the *International Feminist Conference on Women, Law and Social Control:* Quebec, Canada; Feldman, S. & Glen Elliot. (1990). "Progress and promise of research on adolescence." in Feldman, S. & Elliot, G. (Eds.). (1990). *At the threshold: The developing adolescent*. Cambridge: Harvard University Press.

24   Campbell, 1981, cited in Cain, 1989, p. 109 .

[25] Brennan, T. (1980). "Mapping the diversity among runaways." *Journal of Family Issues,* 1(2) , 189-209; Englander, S. (1984). "Some self-reported correlates of runaway behavior in adolescent females." *Journal of Consulting and Clinical Psychology,* 52, 484-5; Horn, M. (1989). *Before It' too late: The child guidance movement in the United States, 1922-1945.* Philadelphia: Temple University Press; Noblit, G. (1976). "The adolescent experience and delinquency." *Youth and Society,* 8 (1), 27-43; Sharlin, S. & Mor-Barak, M. (1992). "Runaway girls in distress: Motivation, background and personality." *Adolescence,* 27 (106), 387-405.

[26] Gaines, D. (1988). *Teenage wasteland suburbias' deadend kids.* New York: Harper Perennial; Gray, E. (1993). *Unequal justice: The prosecution of child sexual abuse.* New York: Free Press; Robertson, Marjorie & Greenblatt, M. (Eds.). (1992). *Homelessness A National Perspective.* New York and London: Plenum Press; Whitbeck, L. & Simons, R. (1990). "Life on the streets: The victimization of runaway and homeless adolesents." *Youth and Society,* 22,(1), 108-120.

[27] Robertson, M. (1989). "Homeless youth: An overview of recent literature". *Monograph of the Alcohol Research Group,* Berkeley: California.

[28] Erickson, E. (1955). "The psychological development of chldren". In J.M. Tanner and B. Inhelder (eds, *Discussion on child development.* Vol. III. New York: Internaton Universities Press, pp. 169-216.

[29] Sharlin, S. & Mor-Barak, M. (1992). "Runaway girls in distress: Motivation, background and personality." *Adolescence,* 27 (106), 387-405.

[30] Sharlin & Mor-Barack, 1992
[31] Sharlin & Mor-Barak, 1992
[32] Sharlin & Mor-Barak, 1992
[33] Takanishi, R. (1978). "Childhood as a social issue: Historical roots of contemporary child advocacy movements." *Journal of Social Issues,* 34 (2), 8-28.

[34] Green & Essellysn, cited in Brennan, T. (1980). "Mapping the diversity among runaways." *Journal of Family Issues,* 1(2) , 189-209.

35 Stierlin, cited in Brennen, 1980.

36 Brennen, 1980, p. 195.

37 Caspi, A., Lynam, D., Moffitt, T. & Silva, P. (1993). "Unraveling girls' delinquency: biological, dispositional and contextual contributions to adolescent misbehavior." *Developmental Psychology*, 29(1), 19-30.

38 Caspi, et al, 1993, p.26

39 Noblit, G. (1976). "The adolescent experience and delinquency." *Youth and Society*, 8 (1), 27-43.

40 Asbury, Herbert (1927). *The gangs of New York: An informal history of the underworld.* Garden City, N.Y. : Garden City Publishing Co; Merton, Robert,K. (1968). *Social theory and social structure.* New York: Free Press; Thrasher, Frederic (1928). *A study of 1303 gangs in Chicago.* Chicago University Press.

41 Gitlin, T. (1987). *The sixties: Years of hope, days of rage.* New York: Bantam Books.; Hall, S. & Jefferson, J. (Eds.). (1989). *Resistance through rituals: Youth subculture in post war Britain.* Boston, London: Unwin Hyman; Hebdige, D. (1979). *Subculture: The meaning of style.* London: Routledge.; Jankowski-Sanchez, M. (1991). *Islands in the street: Gangs and American urban society.* Berkeley: University of California Press.; Sullivan, M. (1989). *Getting paid: Youth and work in the inner city.* New York: Cornell Press.

42 Breines, W. (1992). *Young, white and miserable.* Boston: Beacon Press.; Cain, 1989; Campbell, A. (1984). *Girls in the gang.* (1981). *Girl delinquents.* Oxford: Basil Blackwell; Harris, M. (1988.). *Cholos Latino girls and gangs.* New York: AMS Press.; McRobbie, A. (1989). *Feminism and youth culture.* Boston: Unwin Hyman.; Taylor, C. (1993). *Girls, gangs, women and drugs.* East Lansing: Michigan University Press.

43 (Robeson, 1992)

44 Chesney-Lind, 1991 p.17

45 Chesney-Lind, M. (1989). Girls' crime and woman's place: Toward a feminist model of female delinquency. Crime and Delinquency, 35(1), 5-29.

46 Davis, Angela, (1981). *Women, race and class.* New York: Random House

[47]   Chesney-Lind, 1991

[48]   (Robeson, 1992)

[49]   Proshansky,H., Ittelson, W., & Rivlin, L., (1976). *Environmental psychology,people and their physical settings,* 2nd edition. New York: Holt Rinehart and Winston

[50]   Dryfoos, J. (1990). *Adolescents at risk* . New York: Oxford University Press. p.3

[51]   Fine, M. (1990.). "Who's at risk?" *Journal of Urban and Cultural Studies,* 1(1), 155-168.

[52]   Dryfoos, 1990

[53]   Dryfoos, 1990

[54]   Irwin, 1985

[55]   Douglas, M. (1992). *Risk and blame: Essays in cultural theory* . London: Routledge.

[56]   Dryfoos, 1990

[57]   Campbell, 1984; Hall, 1989; Harris, 1988; Jankowski, 1991

[58]   Fine, 1990

[59]   Ruddick, S. (1988) . "Debunking the dream machine: The case of street kids in Hollywood," CA. Children's *Environment Quarterly* , 5 (1), 8-16.

[60]   Dear, M. & Wolch, J. (1987). *Landscapes of despair.* Princeton: Princeton University Press.

[61]   Stutz, 1987, cited in Ruddick, 1988

[62]   Brockman, cited in Ruddick, 1988, p.12

[63]   Rivlin, L. (1986). "A new Look at homeless." *Social Policy,* Spring, 3-10.

III

The Social Production of Space
Among Punk Girls

This study of environments used by girls who live-on-their-own focuses on San Francisco's downtown: the Civic Center, South of Market and Polk Street neighborhoods. I used a "snowball" sampling technique and interviewed 10 young women using open ended questions. The sample of girls was skewed towards those who either knew each other or had seen each other on the street. Participants were part of a well hidden population to which few adults have access.

CONCEPTUAL FRAMEWORK

The social production of space forms the theoretical and conceptual framework of this chapter, as outlined in great detail by Wolfe and Manzo.[1] Their framework offers a grounded and historical knowledge of space in a contextualized and interpretative history. "As a template for analysis it clarifies the interplay between forces at the present moment and other times, looking for differences as well as similarities; discontinuities as well as continuities; changes in language, use and meaning as well as form" or spatial organization.[2] Understanding people-environment relationships in a moment in time is a complex task which must include an understanding of specific dominant and subcultural social histories, as well as architectural history.

The decision to inhabit abandoned buildings or "squat" is informed by a variety of ideological factors and social histories that impact the production of resources. Age-based restrictions, lack of affordable housing, gender-based moral codes and San Francisco's historic non-conformist communities all legitimize young women's acquisition of space. The beatniks, hippies, Punks and gay and lesbian communities who attempted to find refuge in the supposed tolerance of San Francisco, affect the spatial decisions made by young San Francisco women on their own. The ideological link among young people who identify and belong to a subculture is connected to the social history of San Francisco. The Punks' political ideology, a challenge to the dominant rules of geography, ageism and capitalism, makes sense in a place that historically supports non-conformist and radical political and social activity. In part, young women's decisions are informed by the belief that socially progressive places treat girls with more respect. This belief is refuted in biographies of women who participated in socially progressive movements.[3] However, the investigation of ageism in the power dynamics between adults and young people is not part of any progressive agenda. Social histories are a link to understanding the experiences of resistance and dominance expressed by the young women in this study.

According to Spain, "...the organization of space is both product and producer of existing (and historical) economic relations: spatial representations expressed in their own logic... active instruments in the production and reproduction of the social order."[4] Yet, few social scientists sufficiently address gender, youth subculture, sexuality, mental and physical disability, race and ethnicity in their examination of space .

GENDER IN THE CITY

During the early development of cities, control and surveillance of city life was always directed at women in particular. This is because "...urban life potentially challenged patriarchal systems. With the coming of modernity, the cities of veiled women have ceded to cities of spectacle and voyeurism, in which women while seeking and sometimes finding the freedom of anonymity are often all too visible."[5] Women, even young Punks, are part of the spectacle which brings people to the city. Advertisements and movies which sell "bad women" and their body parts are part of the urban landscape where many of the participants in this study live. The contradictions of social control and "American" consumerism, economic survival and gender/youth exploitation, resistance and paternalism meet on the street. Analyzing and understanding the meaning of these experiences becomes further complicated by racism and youth subcultural style. Gender disorder ideologies, lesbian and gay culture, and student activism of the 1960's permeates both style and ideology of Punk youth subcultures. The complicated nature of understanding young women's experience and its spatial implications can be traced to historical ideas about the development of cities and the conduct of urban life-- controversies which often conceal an underlying morality that women are roaming the streets.

At the turn of the century, "American" novels constructed a gender-based relationship between the wilderness and men and cities and women.[6] For example, in Willa Cather's 'O Pioneers! (1913) the male heroes flees from the materialistic evils of the city to the Edenic frontier in search of their own lost innocence and an "authentic existence." "The female heroines flee from the bareness and torpor of the prairie and the small town to the freedom of the city in search of experience and adulthood."[7] The moral of these stories and others like them, is that the "Man" is separate from, morally superior to, and sovereign over "Mother Nature." Man may tame or exploit Mother Nature, like women, for his own benefit. The dichotomization of cities and wilderness is another cosmological construction in the symbolic universe of male supremacy. Aligned with the opposition of city and country culture is the duality of man as culture and woman as the chaotic earth.

With these early and "worldly" social constructions comes a knowledge of territory for men and women. Certain behaviors are expected in order to maintain the borders of this territory and are linked closely with identity and the judgments we make accordingly. Those who are settled down in a home are stable and trustworthy while those who are unstably housed are vagrants and subject to arrest or fine.[8]

Goffman proposed that gender segregation is fluid: men and women periodically separate into different places but re-group in integrated spaces to carry out shared goals.[9] Thorne cites gender segregation in schools as a component of childhood development for boys and girls.[10] Ardener's extensive anthropological collection of articles highlight the importance of spatial arrangement and women.[11] Rosaldo proposed nearly twenty years ago that women's status is lowest in societies with highly differentiated private and public spheres.[12] Thus the greater the distance between women and girls and the sources of valued knowledge, the greater the gender stratification.[13]

In contradiction to the above theories, Katz studied girls in a small village in the Sudan and in other urban cities in the United States.[14] She indicated that purdah, the culturally based separation of boys and girls in Muslim societies, does not inhibit girls' activities in the environment as much as fear-based rules among parents in the United States. Thus, girls in urban cities of the United States are more restricted than girls under the rules of purdah in the Sudan. Piche's study of girls contradicts Katz's study.[15] The girls in her study living in public housing did not feel restricted in their access to the environment. In fact, they would go wherever they could find peers, and did not go where there were groups of people with whom they did not identify. The lack of opportunities offered to girls in the public realm does differ from boys; they often join their male friends in activities as a defense against the sexual harassment they experience in public spaces. The small apartment space in public housing affords young women little indoor space for gatherings. The use of boys as a defense, available to girls in the United States, may not be available to girls in Muslim countries. Thus, the contradiction of boys as both sexual aggressors and protectors is a dialectic which most girls confront while trying to survive. When indoor space is limited due to poverty or parental restrictions, outdoor space is used extensively and in varied ways. The factors that guide the use of the environment for girls, including fear, is more complex and varied then discussed in Katz's article.

Incorporating an analysis of the social production of space reveals how both historical and current relations are constituted and experienced among young women-on-their-own. These factors, however, are often invisible due to omission in research studies. Focusing on invisibility leads to the discovery of other invisible relationships. Clues to the structural maintenance of subordination and dominance is embedded in the experiences of young Punk women living-on-their-own.

The contemporary girl squatters resist the gender-based urban dichotomies of the last century. They fight for their right to shelter, which can also be coded as the freedom to be a girl on-her-own. The squatting Punk girl's ideology places shelter rights over property rights. Confrontations with the police (authority) and adult homeless groups who would take their shelters from them is the 1996 version of resisting the worldly construction of men and women, adults and youth. Girls on-their-own confront the borders of both private and public territory that maintains social control.

A GEOGRAPHY OF RISK

All of the young women I interviewed for this study hang out in the Downtown area (including Polk Street, the Tenderloin and Civic Center) and develop squats in the South of Market district. When asked why they go South of Market to squat, they responded that they wanted to get out of the "mix" in the Tenderloin or Civic Center. The "hustling" environment is loud, demanding and dangerous, not the kind of place where one can rest and get some peace and quiet.

Half the young women in this study were raised in San Francisco. However, local residency did not mean that the participants had a bigger cognitive map of San Francisco than the girls who were recent inhabitants. Most of them had been to, and know how to get to the Haight area (2 miles from downtown) and Castro (1.5 miles from downtown). They venture out to the beach in the most western part of the city and also the Embarcadero, a tourist area located near the periphery of downtown along the edge of the bay. These were the only neighborhoods in which the young women stayed. The Castro is an area for panhandling late at night, after the bars close at 2 am. Young women rarely sleep in this area because there are few abandoned buildings. Many of the young women feel safe there because the men are gay and do not want to exploit them sexually. Longer excursions included going to the beach. The Beach area is a place to hang out and relax for the day. Though some of the young women thought they might live there for a while, they often do not stay for more than a few days before returning to the Civic Center. They feel the beach was too far away from friends and needed supplies, like food, and there are few abandoned buildings near the beach. Locating a secure shelter is a time consuming activity.

> Interviewer: How did you find the squat?
> Theresa: I found squats myself. You just walk around sometimes you go squat hunting. The only time I ever find squats is when I'm not looking for one, though you know. Like coming back from somewhere, walking on a weird street that you don't usually walk on and there's an abandoned building and you scope it out for a couple of days.
> I: What do you look for?
> Theresa: It has to look abandoned most of all. Look for no one coming in or out, ever. Look for a doorway or window you can get in and out easily most of the time with no seeing you, like in a back alley or something What some squatters do is put a lock on a door and see what happens, if it gets fucked with they know that they can't do it. But if it doesn't they know they can move in. Usually you should watch it for a week. It's not a good idea to find a place and sleep in it the next day unless you have nowhere else to go. Then you just say fuck it and do it.

The young women in this study squat hunt during the day, often climbing up unsafe fire escapes, or up to the roof to find an entry into a closed building. It is not safe to stay the night in a squat found that day. Putting a lock on the front door

for a few days ensures that the building is not inhabited by
other squatters or watched by the owner. If the lock is still on
the door a few days later, it's a good squat. Depending on the
type of building, most girls stay in a room with other squatters
and often have their "best girlfriends" or boyfriends sleep with
them in the bed. Homophobia within squats creates additional
risks. A number of girls did not tell their friends their sexual
feelings towards other girls because they did not want to
jeopardize their tenancy in the squat.

All of the young women who participated in this study
thought that their contacts with the police were the most
dangerous encounters while on-their-own. Often police "bust a
squat" in the middle of the night, with dogs and flashlights,
chasing squatters from roof top to roof top. The young women's
possessions are usually ready to go at a moments notice. Sadness
(16 years old), who had been living on her own for 3 years, had
a pet rabbit. During a squat bust police told her the next time
they caught her, she would be arrested and her rabbit given to
the Animal Control Unit (a place where stray animals are
killed). The average length of stay at any squat is about one to
two weeks, before the squat is busted. There are few activists
fighting with these young people for their right to shelter.
Without policy changes which address the lack of shelter
rights for youth-on-their-own, young women will continue to
run from the police at 2 am. The implications of this policy are
nothing less than danger and death.

> Betty: This is a nine story squat that we lived in on
> the top floors. I've had a lot of fun. We lived in this
> squat when the war demonstrations were going on, the
> anti-war demonstrations. We would sit upstairs and
> have all these political discussion by candlelight.
> We went in the front door.

In the summer of 1992, a 15 year old woman who was squatting
in this building fell nine stories through the elevator shaft and
will never walk again. Few people squat there any longer, out
of respect for this young woman, but as fewer and fewer

buildings remain standing in the face of urban gentrification, some young women are left with no choice.

Despite their lack of housing stability, many of the young women in this study attempted to return to school. All of the young women wanted to return to school and some did even when they were squatting. Most of the young women had left school when they were just approaching their teenage years. At that time, school just didn't seem to work for them anymore.

> I: How come you left school?
> Mary: I just transferred from Packer. Packer is a really small farmer town and Belling was a big redneck town and uh I like transferred. I was not doing good in school and my mom told me I was stupid so I should just quit. One day it just all got to me and found out I was flunking band and I'm like, I've always been really good in band. I was in solo and ensemble and stuff and I can play flute really good and I couldn't understand why I was flunking but I guess it was because I didn't go to a prep assembly or whatever, and anyway, I just said fuck you and I dropped out like two seconds later and I went home and said oh by the way I dropped out, Mom. She said, Oh, I knew you would.

Mary returned to school, as do many of the young women, even when they have nowhere to stay.

> I: Were you in School when you were squatting?
> Mary: I'd been going to school since December it was crazy. We took the elevator to the very top floor and turned it off and slept there and got pretty good sleeping til 6 or 7 the next morning. This guy opened it up with a crowbar and said you better get out and thought he was going to beat the shit out of us.

The issues of safety, freedom and protection are critical issues for all women in day-to-day life. "Women have a right to the carnival, intensity and even the risks of the city. ...urban

life, however fraught with difficulty, has emancipated women
more than rural life or suburban domesticity."[16] Unfortunately,
many girls are trained in our society to expect and accept
spatial limitations. They are taught to occupy but not control
space, keep their self and social boundaries permeable. As
youth, girls are to tolerate the decisions of adults. As adults,
women are supposed accept frequent interruptions by their
children and husbands or male co-workers and bosses. Most boys
grow up on the streets where they learn the lessons of manhood.
"Nice girls" are kept off the streets and close to the home, lest
their virginity or virtue become endangered.[17]

While advertisements, catcalls and whistles may attempt
to define and control them, girls and women find spatial
freedom in the city, inspite of the confines of socially
constructed norms of female space, control and socialization.

> I: What was that like in Seattle?
> Digy: It was OK I mean I got hassled by people but
> not any more than usual. If you're panhandling on the
> street, older men will come and try to pick you up. At
> least 20 times a day. They think because you're a kid
> and you're poor that you're going to do it.

Privacy for women on the streets is violated no matter how
well you learn to handle intrusions. Areas like the Tenderloin,
Civic Center, Downtown, and South of Market are filled with
porno-movie and book stores, pictures of dismembered women
and scenes of women having sex with women for the pleasure of
men. The continual message is that men are powerful and
women can be consumed, controlled, raped and dehumanized.

> I: Since you left home have you been in any risky or
> dangerous situations?
> Theresa: I didn't think that walking down the street
> was a risky situation but I got here, it's rough on Turk
> Street; people just fuck with you. Someone just sort of
> beat me up just cause I was walking down the street
> and didn't like how I looked, they didn't like how
> my friend looked so he tried to light her hair on fire

and I pushed his arm out of the way which I guess I shouldn't have done (laugh). My first reaction was to just push his arm out of the way so he when I was walking away I was like why are you doing this you don't know us I never said anything to you. We started walking away and he ran up behind us and punched me on the side on the head like my jaw hurt for weeks. It's kind of risky just walking down the street.

Unfortunately, the street provides an economy for young women to earn money for an occasional hotel room, when squatting becomes too difficult and overwhelming.

Sadness: I have a fake ID and I can strip for a living.
I: Have you done that before?
Sadness: Yeah, I've done it once in Seattle, and its not that big of a deal and I can make a lot of money really fast and maybe I can get my own apartment or move into someone else's. I'm tired of people's little games. Most of the time it's good but sometimes it gets really rotten.

For young women, resisting, negotiating and surviving both the violence of the streets and their poverty renders them "autonomous." Only in the secrecy of their squats and in certain neighborhoods, do these young women have a place to discuss their values, ideas and projects that do not conform to the dominant social interest.

Patesha: You are going to have people look at you and feel more sorry for you because you are a girl on the street than if you are a guy. You gonna have people try to take you in and use you and try to play you for a fool. You are gonna have trouble if you're trying to sell drugs because they think females don't know what they are talking about. If you try to prostitute on your own if that's what you do to get your money, girls might get ripped off, abused, beaten. I think if you're a strong willed female and you take care of yourself and watch out for yourself or have friends who will watch your back, it's not much different, you're just a minority, you're street kid, you're trash. But there are a lot of butch girls on the street and nobody messes with them."

LINKING SQUATS TO THEIR SPATIAL HISTORIES

Squatting is historically linked to European colonialists, housing activists, Hippies, European Punks and homelessness.[18] United State's squat history is related to the unequal distribution of land and wealth, dating back to the early colonialist squatters.[19] Embedded in an understanding of squatting is the concept of property rights. The institutions developed to legalize tenancy subsequently undermined and devastated the Native American cultures, justifying the sale and theft of native lands. Europeans were all squatters in the "New Land". In the 1830's, the debate over homesteading or squatting was regional, embedded in the political and social differences between the north and the south (agrarian and industrial) and the east and west "pioneers". By the 1850's, squatters grew rebellious as surveyors put "their" land on the auction block at prices squatters could seldom afford. Squatters began to block land sales to the railroads by forming land organizations. The Homestead Act of 1862 currently protects squatters in New York City. It was the first law affording women property rights, but specifically promoted heterosexual marriage by rewarding husband and wife with twice as much land as a single person.[20]

The rent strikes of the mid and late 19th and 20th centuries provide another historical link to squatting. Rent strikes laid the groundwork for tenant unions and mass strikes, evident today in many cities. The 1904 rent strikes, conducted along lines of workplace strikes, used the tactics of withholding rent, stopping evictions and organizing picket lines to keep eviction crews out of buildings. "Thus the 19th and 20th century rent strike activity in urban centers links the early frontier squatting and the activity of 150 to 200 years later."[21]

Squatting in the United States is rarely recognized and poorly understood. There has never been legal housing available to young women on their own. The legal constraints that preclude young women from signing leases and contracts, working without consent of their parents, being on the street after curfew, making decisions about their lives and living outside the sanctity of the "family unit" are not yet political issues being challenged. Throughout the last century, young girls have been placed in group and foster homes, or institutionalized in other ways. To include young women in the category of homelessness clouds both the ideological and economic issues which surround their situation. "Street girls" represent a resistance to ideologies involving the social control of young women and challenge the production and use of space in urban areas from a class and gender perspective. Girls on-their-own force the realization that Punks and other youth subcultures create knowledge and use space in an counter-hegemonic fashion. It is this complex interplay which constitutes the social production of space for young women on their own.

The discussion of homelessness in this country is predominantly related to adults, and more recently, children within families. Rarely does it refer to young people on their own. Social scientists rely on historical and economic circumstances and individual pathology to explain the causes of "homelessness." The generally accepted causes of homelessness do not apply to young people. The typical reasons for homelessness, discussed in the literature are: lack of affordable low-income housing and loss of jobs. The death of a spouse or battering, as well as physical illness and lack of health care insurance, often leads to women's homelessness. For young people, the literature cites the following reasons for homelessness: abusive and neglectful parents, rebellion, drug use and general juvenile delinquent behaviors such as pregnancy or having sex with the same sex.[22] Youth-at-risk policy developers, service providers and researchers rarely highlight lack of affordable housing as a root of unstable housing. Based on the dominant research, young women-on-their own are the product of individual pathologies within a family structure. While this may be partly true, the larger structural problems that are meaningful factors for young women on their own and are integral to the social production of squats are lost in currently accepted social science theories and knowledge.

In studying the patterns of homeless youth in Hollywood, Ruddick argues that the dynamics of homeless youth geography are not understood because homeless youth are spatially segregated from homeless adults.[23] Thus, locating services in "traditional haunts of homeless adults may not best serve the needs of homeless and runaway youth." Many of the youth in her study (3 females and 12 males) stated that they preferred to be in areas of Hollywood where adult homeless people do not congregate. They did not feel safe in those areas, due to violence from homeless adults, other gangs, and police.

Ruddick's earlier work (pre-Los Angeles uprising) unravels the dynamics of homeless and runaway youth geography and asserts that the issue of service provision is confounded with discourse about redevelopment. After the uprising, Ruddick sees the issue of homeless youth in Hollywood submerged in a debate which hides the racialization of Los Angeles redevelopment.[24] In comparison to South Central, Hollywood has been able to raise millions of dollars for services for "homeless youth." Hollywood's redevelopment and the subsequent destruction of squats is occurring almost as quickly as squats are found. Yet, youth are not leaving Hollywood. There are other factors, such as services, the underground economy, and the presence of youth subculture which continue to attract youth-on-their-own to Hollywood. However, finding creative and secure shelter is now more time-consuming.

THE SOCIAL PRODUCTION OF NEIGHBORHOODS WHERE SQUATS EXIST

There are many neighborhoods in San Francisco where African American, Latino, Asian/Pacific Islander including Samoan,

Cambodian, Philipino, Chinese and White young people hang out and work in the street economies. "Homeless" white youth are visible on the street in the Haight Ashbury and Downtown (including Polk Street, The Tenderloin and Civic Center). While many of the study participants initially lived in the Haight Ashbury neighborhood, they later moved downtown where they found different opportunities. Downtown offers a variety of youth subcultures, cheaper food, more tourists to panhandle, more buildings to squat, and youth outreach and drop-in services.

> Doherty: First I was living on Haight street with some chick in her apartment. There were 20 of us all squatting in her apt. and that was a rad scene. There was one bedroom, tiny apartment, 30 people every night on Haight Street and everyone was dirty and smelled and it was worse than my apartment is right now, 10 times worse. I'm serious. It was so nasty, stuff on the floor. We would just panhandle for burritos. Panhandling used to be really good up there. I used to make like 10 bucks in 45 minutes like no problem. Now I go up there and I can't even make like a dollar in fucking 2 hours.
> I: Why?
> Doherty:I think I look old, I don't look like I'm 15 anymore, yeah like you have money, I don't please, please. And then I started squatting up on Haight by Polytech. I squatted there for a while. I started going out with another dude and he hung out downtown. I had never hung out downtown and I'd like OK I'll go down there with you and like that's when I found Larkin Street and Hospitality House and the fact that beer was so much cheaper and everything was so much cheaper in the Tenderloin than in the Haight and it was easier to panhandle down here and there weren't so many yuppies and fucking stiff assholes. It was cool, like I could hang out here, everyone is a scum bag, cool, rad."

The differences found by Doherty in these two neighborhoods is partly due to the social, economic, racial and development patterns in San Francisco. Many white young women who leave "home" and arrive in San Francisco initially go to the Haight Ashbury Golden Gate Park, whose history as a bohemian enclave is over a century old. Whether the young women know it or not, they are following a long tradition. In the 1860's, the Golden Gate Park was planned to extend further to the east and across much of the Haight Ashbury but a number of squatters in the area could not be dislodged."[25] For eighty years, the Haight remained somewhat suburban. This changed once cars became widely owned and the real suburbs were developed, leaving places like the Haight to become more citified. During the 1950's the Haight did not experience the same blight as the South of Market, Tenderloin or Mission Districts due to large redevelopment projects in the adjacent Fillmore neighborhood. Displaced African American working class people moved to the Haight along with beatniks from North Beach. A number of social and economic events made the Haight ripe for the "hippie era", including a neighborhood identity of common transience and a long-standing liberal community tolerance of alternative lifestyles. The Haight was also the common living area of many rock and roll stars including The Grateful Dead, Jefferson Starship, Janis Joplin, Jimi Hendrix, as well as the home of a subcultural philosophy opposed to the pursuit of material affluence. Almost overnight, the Haight Ashbury became a mecca for disenchanted youth from all over America, who occupied flats or just slept in the park. The *SF Examiner* wrote the following anti-counter cultural account in 1969:

> Some of the crash pads of the streets- once neatly maintained dwellings are foul litter-infested, evil smelling latrines. Dog feces, festering garbage and broken bottles abound next to living establishments that are meticulously maintained. It is from many of the hovels that the predatory types emerge at night- like hungry rats to loot, forage and violate. [26]

Neighborhood change, including the displacement of low income people in San Francisco, generally follows political, economic and social forces of "bohemian influx, middle-class transition and bourgeois consolidation."[27] Thus, a non-conformist population discovers a neighborhood, making a "dangerous" or rundown neighborhood livable and attractive to others who would not normally walk down the street. The word gets out, housing speculation begins and the entrepreneurial class moves in. Businesses representing bourgeois consolidation enter the area, catering to a wealthier class. Rents rise. The population becomes more homogenous and the original bohemians move away or remain in the neighborhood but move out of their bohemian phase and into a more affluent economic class. [28] There are few non-gentrified residential areas left in San Francisco. Downtown redevelopment has drastically changed the landscape of the traditional transient neighborhood of South of Market area. Squats are being destroyed daily, leaving fewer places for young women to find shelter.

The planning and development objectives outlined in "The San Francisco Master Plan" acknowledge the "valuable low cost rental housing" in the area including the Civic Center, Tenderloin neighborhoods, and South of Market District. [29] There are approximately 10,000 (reported) residents living in 5,000 dwelling units (including apartments, flats and hotels), not including artists living in industrial buildings and an unknown number of "street people" who reside in various forms of "spontaneous shelters." The estimated number of homeless people living in San Francisco is 10,000.[30] The planning report states that "The City of San Francisco seems content with the residential quality and number of dwellings available. The stock matches the space and needs and housing affordabililty levels of existing residents."[31] In contradiction, homeless youth, and young women in particular, are not content with the residential dwellings available.

> Betty: Over here, these garages, is where we used to sneak in. This one down here, see, they have boards in them now they were always opened a little and we

would crawl underneath. This is where I got staph infection from all the glass and the dirt. I used to have cuts all over my hands full of staff infection. There were like 30 or 40 people here. And like some floors were just warehouse with a couple of rooms around the sides. I loved this squat. I stayed here for like 2 months. Off and on, I stayed there and we went to Seattle and I came back and stayed here again. My room in here was so rad Oh my god. It was a loft and it was boxes around the loft and it looked just like a shelf but it had a ladder I could pull up and I hid it under the staircase. It was my own room. Basically it didn't look like a room. The police would come in and we would all hide in my room because to the cops, it just looked like a shelf, but I could stand up and not hit my head on the ceiling cause the ceiling was so high. It's an old party goods party favor factory.

Since 1970, the population of San Francisco has remained about the same while the number of housing units available to rent has increased. In 1990 there were 5, 492 more vacant units than in 1980. A total of 22, 887 units of housing were vacant. San Francisco is still a city of renters, as two-thirds of the city population rents. The number of people living with more than one person per room doubled from 1980 to 1990, indicating that the number of vacant units does not provide more space per person. As the number of available squats decreases, a new mixture of people and cultures are forced to share squats.

On 7th Street:
Betty: This is the Greyhound Building, but it's attached to a hotel. We would walk through where the Greyhound part was but we lived in the hotel part and the hotel on the right on top. I would go there by myself and carry this pen with me. Piss and shit everywhere. Floors with dead pigeons we

couldn't stay on. I'll show you how we got in. Oh my
god there were 150 people living here.

According to the South of Market District Report, 15% of
the population live in households containing three or more
persons.[32] This represents twice as much crowding in the South
of Market area than in the city as a whole. The rent prices for
the South of Market are lower than those for the city as a
whole, and the median income for South of Market households
was less than half the citywide median income level in 1980.
The plan promotes specific policy objectives for this area:
"...to convert the existing housing to residential zones,
protecting it from industrial or business conversions as well as
maintain the low rents and the current tenancy who could not
afford the rents in other parts of the city." In contrast to these
objectives, the plan allows for "...the development of housing
without adversely affecting the scale, density, and
architectural character of the neighborhoods and the
conversion of abandoned single room occupancy hotels to be
converted to low income units as well as limit the number of
liquor stores along 6th street.[33]
    Sixth street (South of Market) is a hub for transient and
homeless residents of the area, and while liquor stores are not
"desirable" as the only commercial activity, they provide
many needed administrative neighborhood services to people
who would otherwise have no "legitimate" business contacts.
Liquor stores cash checks and offer convenient supplies. In the
1980's, as the South of Market buildings decreased in number,
the contrast between the "downtown" and the South of Market
urban landscape increased. The new developments represent
parking lots and corporate office plazas where low income
housing and single room occupancy housing used to exist.

> Betty: This is it, the squat. I lived here for six
> months. It's been a parking lot for like 2 years. I loved
> it, we had electricity, running water, TVs. I had my
> own room with a single, double bed and dresser, three
> stories. We got in through the front door. I guess it
> was an apartment building ,something like that. An

apartment building where some of it was like one
room apartments. I don't know maybe it was like flats
or something. Because there would be like a room and
a bathroom in the hallway. It wasn't a hotel. I think
it was like just a bunch of flats. There were probably
about 20 people living in the building or 30. We used
to have big dinners together and everyone was doing
something, panhandling or selling pot or something
and we chipped in and had dinner together. It was
one of the most organized squats I've ever lived in
that I was a member of, you know.

Young women want only to have a secure living environment
with no restrictions, such as curfews or other moralistic rules
regarding sex and sexuality. In order to find that in San
Francisco, they must maneuver around the new building
developments which take away shelter opportunities and do
not provide job opportunities. Betty recalls the shelters they
used to have:

Betty: All these lots were all warehouses that we
lived in. There were maybe six warehouses. Now flat
ground, flat land of nothingness, hundreds of people
could be living but we're more worried about parking
places. Basically we'd scope them out and figure out
how we were going to get in through the back. Once in
a while there were garage doors, there were lots of
them so whenever we got kicked out of one we'd move
to another. Damn, some of them had electricity, some
of them were very styling. I don't know, this sucks
man.

LOCAL GEOGRAPHIC MYTHOLOGY

I: Do most squats have mythology about them?
Patesha: Yeah, a lot of the squatters start it because
they don't want other squatters to go there. But this
was real because they have this Satan symbol and I
mean blood marks on the wall. If you walked down to
the basement and walked this hallway, different
spots were cold and warm..."

Myths are powerful agents of social control. According to
environmental psychologist, S. Klein, "myths seek to
legitimate dominant ideologies.[34] Myths change the socially
constructed into the seemingly inevitable. Myth presents the
social scientist with a role and a problematic: to decipher,
decode and deconstruct myths; and to reconstruct alternatives to
them". [35] Klein's study uses the concept of myth, as defined by
Barthes, to understand the context for creating and using myths
and to define the idealized image of the bourgeois world. [36]
    Myths also function to pass on information within
marginalized groups in order to maintain the cultural
knowledge (almost secretively) among their group members.
The tales told by the young women about spaces accomplishes
many things. Sometimes the stories grant them license to
occupy a building or create fear about physical safety based on
unstated but known structural damage. The myths provide
historical architectural information, chart previous occupants,
building use and hiding places. This "alternative neighborhood
history" challenges the established knowledge and evolution
of a neighborhood and its structures. The myths gave multiple
meanings to the geography. If two or more realities could exist
at the same time, the myth pointed to the complexity of
spatial decisions made among these young women, and revealed
another invisible border separating us. I could not see what
they saw when they looked at a building, street, or
neighborhood.

Betty was 14 when she began living on her own. She was born in San Francisco and had squatted in many buildings. The social and "underground" tenant history of one of the first squats she stayed in is described below:

Betty: This squat is remains of a humongous school. Someone built condos. On either side they built condos and we squatted in the remaining girls gym. So basically we got busted because people in the condos saw us going in and out.

I: How did you get in?

Betty: This is a really old squat that a lot of people have lived in (It was first opened in the 1970's). When it was first opened people were staying in the principal's office and stuff. When it was first opened before they tore part of it down. We were the second generation of people living here because we lived in here after, it was pretty much trashed. It was a pretty gross squat. There were no boards there (she's pointing to a window in a small yard) we could open the window to the basement and we crawled through the windows, jumped down onto the sink and like could only get in (she's out of breath) Used to be blackberry bushes all over here and we could pick them in the morning when we woke up. On the ground there were blackberry bushes. We slept up there (the second floor). I can see an anarchy sign up there (inside on the wall). This was our bedroom, all the windows were shot out. They were all gone (there are windows in the building now). We came in here the very first time we ever broke in, (through the side door). In the first room there was electricity but there was supposed to be this really old hermit that will like, kill you if you step into his building. Wow, yep and there's the gym, we used to walk up those stairs right there. There's another anarchy sign, oh yeah, that's someone's room. Swastika there, I know because there are a lot of skin heads that used to squat. (Sigh) There were a hell of swastikas here

when we first came here and found a burned baby doll
in the middle of the gym. It was really freaky, we got
all freaked out and graffittied over everything so we
would feel rad about living there. It was pretty
freaky when we first came in. I opened this squat for
the second time.

Sorry was 16 years old, and had been on her own for two
years. In that time, she had developed a system of finding
squats and an intuitive sense of what constituted a safe squat.

Sorry: I was squatting all over, but there was one
main one. I don't want to explain all the others, it
was the same idea. I'm squatting right now, but we
got busted so I'm looking for a new one for tonight. We
found one but it's scary. I think the South of Market
Murderer lives there because it said "red rum" on the
wall in red drippy writing. It was this weird murder
writing on the bottom. We just ran out. I never get the
creeps from abandoned buildings because I've lived in
so many. But from when we first walked in that place
it looked creepy.

Theresa came to San Francisco because the winters in New
York City were too difficult. She had heard that there were
strong girls in San Francisco. She describes the squat she lived
in for over a year-and-a-half in New York City.

Theresa: I found out about the squat from my friend
who was from my home town. She got me into it. She
had her own room and we shared it. There were 20
people in the squat during the summer, but it was too
cold in the winter. My friend told me that it had been
a squat for two years, first it was a junkie squat, like a
shooting gallery, everybody bought and sold there.
Then someone took it over and it was established as
the PEST squat that stands for Planet, Eggs Scum
Tribe. I lived there for a year or so and then moved

out here. I haven't been a squat longer then two weeks
since I've been in San Francisco.

PUNK CULTURE

Messages are delivered to girls which tell them that Punk
culture will embrace their desire for escape and help them
survive. There is meaning in Punk style, hidden messages that
interrupt the socialization process. Punks seek out disapproval
from the "mainstream" and challenge the basic tenets of
cleanliness, literacy, and decency. Punks offer a social place for
girls who want to escape. Punk girls can experience hedonism
and live a relatively "adult-free life", though not one free of
gender politics.

The squats are generally organized by young men who
identify as Punks or "Grungies." While it is unclear if all the
males have more social status then the young women, it is
evident from the interviews that the assignment of rooms and
sleeping locations is generally decided by a male, even though
explicit squat "rules" defy a hierarchy of any kind. In
contradiction to Punk ideology, a critique of the "feminine and
masculine role" in mainstream society (primarily through
fashion, music and anarchist politics), indicate that girls have
less rights in the squats. While squatting is ideologically based
in a "right to shelter", the social organization of squats is often
(though not always) embedded in a hierarchy informed by
sexism. This hierarchy permeates personal relationships and
can leave a young woman without an expected roof over her
head because her "old man" is using "their" bed with someone
else. Creating equal spaces and rights to spaces among young
men and young women remains a theoretical construct.

The role of the male as spatial organizer of the squat is
particularly detrimental to a young lesbian. Two of the young
women I interviewed felt that they could not have sex with
other women while "living on the street" because they would be
stigmatized by the people in their squat. The fear of
homophobic repercussion kept these women in the closet until

they were in a group home and lesbian foster home, respectively.

Ironically, Punk culture and its discourse provides theoretical options to sleep with boys or girls, allowing for freedom of sexual expression. Along with sexual demands, there are behavioral guidelines around the use of intravenous drug use. In the mainstream, girls who drink and have sex are considered "dangerous" while boys who drink and have sex are being boys. Even in Punk subculture, young women are expected to maintain an allegiance to their men, regardless of their sexual demands or junkie behaviors. Young women are pressured to use drugs or at least tolerate them among their sexual partners and friends. Often , the young women in this study were nursing others and helping them through hard times (bad dope or lack of it). There was always the fear of being evicted from the squat by their friends. My research contrasts with one of the few critical studies of youth subcultures and girls' places within them. In her 1980 article, McRobbie lays out a feminist analysis of the theoretical canons of youth subculture and draws the conclusion that there is little more "freedom" for girls in Punk culture than staying "at home."[37] All the girls in this study identify as Punks and experience more gender and sexual freedom on their own than at home. Though this study focuses on the environmental territories mapped out and used by girls in San Francisco, the gender politics of their youth subcultures developed in squats and on the street is a transitory and pragmatic freedom for young women. Their freedom is different from the sedentary nature of "home". The young women have responsibilities to their "street family." They are often in charge of the logistics of finding an illegal building. At the same time, these girls are exploited by the "male street culture", the gendered, racial and class-biased downtown corporate and tourist milieu. The Punk subculture provides an ideological framework to engage in these dialectical relationships.

The history of Punk subculture, both in England and the United States, provides a framework for understanding the importance of Punk to the young women finding and using spaces in San Francisco. In his history of Punk, Hebdige explains:

> David Bowie's glitter rock was woven together with
> elements from American proto-Punk (the Ramones,
> the Heartbreakers, Iggy Pop, Richard Hell) with
> factions within London pub-rockers (the 101ers)
> inspired by the mod subculture of the 60's from the
> Canvey Island 40's revival and the Southend R & B
> bands, from the north soul and from reggae.[38]

Glam rock contributed narcissism, nihilism and gender confusion. American Punk offered a minimalist aesthetic, the cult of the street and a penchant for self-laceration. "Northern Soul (an underground British subculture of working-class young people dedicated to acrobatic dancing and fast North American soul of the 60's) brought its subterranean tradition of fast, jerky rhythms."[39] The alliance of diverse music was equally matched by its fashion, producing a style which "reproduced the same kind of cacophony on the visual level."[40] Punk fashion is a catalogue of all the post-war subcultures, split apart and pinned together in every imaginable and unimaginable combination. Although many of the Punk parents like David Bowie were not liberated in any radical sense, never transcending sexual role play, they did question the value and meaning of adolescence and the transition to the adult world of work.[41] They confounded the images of men and women and distorted the traditional passage from childhood to maturity. Punks claimed to speak for the neglected constituency of the white lumpen youth. Their obsession with class and relevance was expressly designed to undercut the intellectual posturing of the previous generation of rock musicians. Punks created a cultural space for the crisis of modern life- a "condition of unmitigated exile."[42] There was a strong pull by some Punks towards reggae music and Rastafarianism. The Mohawk hairstyle was in fact a take off on Black dreadlock styles. The English Punks wore Ethiopian colors, creating Rock against Racism, a political movement combating the growing influence of the National Front in working class areas.

United States Punk was born in 1979, and was barely recognized as a youth resistance movement, despite its anti-war and anti-nuke politics.[43] Punks were a new generation of youth, critical of society, and coming into their individuality during a politically repressive time with first hand experience and insights.

I: How long were you living with your girlfriend?
Blue: Four to six months I'm not sure, cause we broke up but we stayed together- which was ridiculous - but we did it anyway. She's way older. She's 22, she's cool. She's a scientist, a Punk Rock scientist. She works with AZT and DDI so, but it wasn't working out.

I: Do you consider yourself a Punk?
Doherty: I consider myself, I guess you could call me a Punk because Punk rock it's just being yourself and don't give a fuck. I don't know there are some Punk rockers out there, some grungies, they're into getting dirty and being vegetarian and stuff. One with the scum.

Sabrina: I had cane and I was all Punk rocker
I: What does that mean?
Sabrina: No, I mean, by the time I came back from SF (arrived in Utah) I was like fuck you, cause everyone there is like really stupid and there Punk rock and I was really annoyed and everyone was like you're so Punk rock. Everyone there lives with their parents and have all these expensive Punk rock clothing. The first night I was there I was drunk with my cane and sitting in the corner. People are like ay what's your name and who's that? That's Sabrina, Oh, what happened to her and I was like nothing, I'm drunk. Where did you come from? SF today and I'm all fucked up. They were all skin heads. This girl Liz is like four of me, four of me, huge big bad bitch. I was talking to her kind of, but I was all drunk (Laughs).
I: So when you say you were really Punk rock, what does that mean?
Sabrina: I was really grungie, and I was more SF style, more I didn't look like a death rocker or anything. You

knew that I was some grungie person who didn't live
with my parents, (Laughs).

I: If you looked like a death rocker what would you
look like?
Sabrina: I would have makeup on, a lot of more quote
un quote "gothic". I don't know how to explain it. But I
was just grungie and my attitude was fuck you people
and I hated everybody and they were stupid. I hated
Utah and all these people.

In the 1980's a Punk scene spread throughout the United
States. "Although the big cities and college towns remained
important sites, it was spreading to the boonies and suburban
metropolitan areas."[44] Radio shows multiplied and unlikely
places in Utah, Texas and Maine had strong Punk scenes,
varying in size from a few dozen to a few thousand. Punks were
not the only youth subculture whose population was expanding.
In San Francisco, different youth subcultures can co-exist
literally across the street from each other.

Patesha: I started hanging out with Punk rockers.
I: Who were you hanging out with before?
Patesha: The gangster crowd. They are just these drug
dealer kind of people. They're supposed to be hard
core with guns in their belts and knives and they just
think they are it.
I: Youth or adults?
Patesha: Both, more like early twenties. Well,
hardly anyone is from San Francisco. They hung out
at Civic Center. The Punk rockers are on the wall,
Carl's Jr.s was the place to be. The gangsters are
around the Civic Center because they sold crack,
speed they were down in the Tenderloin. They hang
across the street from where the Punk rockers hang, in
front of McDonalds, or they'll go in Carl's Jr.s.
I: Girls and boys?
Patesha: Yeah.

I: What is the difference between gangsters and the
Punk rockers?
Patesha: I mean it's a whole different scene, different
spirit, different kind of things you know, just totally
different. These people are these big bad people who
think they can kick everybody's ass, and a lot of the
Punk rockers are like really hyper cause they're on
drugs most of the time. They are really hyperactive,
people, and they can be violent but they don't walk
around like they are it. They are just being different.
When I was hanging with gangsters I was different, I
was cold, I didn't have any feelings at all and when I
was a Punk rocker I was into chaos and mark on things
and squat and just kind of be kind of crazy.
I: Can you have sex with girls if you are a gangster?
Patesha: No, girls cannot have sex with girls. No, I
would have got my ass kicked.

The American Punk scene was anti-1960's nostalgia,
"apocalypse was central to early Punk's symbolic mythology."[45]
Punk announced its disaffection from both middle and working
class standards and U.S. Punks did not ally themselves with
people of color and their music as British did. However,
offshoots of U.S. Punk did challenge the white male dominance
of Punk culture producing independent publications (fanzines)
including *Rock against Racism* and *Rock against Sexism*. The
Rock against Reagan tour, brought together Yippies and other
politicized youth cultures. *Rock against Sexism* was published
out of Boston in the 1980's by a group of lesbian Punks. Their
intent was to raise the consciousness of musicians, listening
audiences, and the music industry to sexist traditions in
rock'n'roll. Their objectives were to support women's non-sexist
bands and to provide comfortable playing, listening and
dancing space for people who didn't like or were denied
entrance to most of the clubs due to age, race, sexuality or price.
Rock against Sexism promoted rock'n'roll alternatives to music
that offends women, gays and lesbians, bisexuals and people of
color. Workshops and information exchanges for women were
held in order to demystify equipment, technology and the music

industry and provided networking opportunities for progressive, political and musical groups in Boston.[46]

In 1984, the first San Francisco Punk protest emerged around the Livermore Anti-Nuclear Action Group's "Hall of Shame Tour" which took place in San Francisco's financial district. Activists condemned financial institutions for participating in and supporting the proliferation of nuclear power. Punks walked in the middle of the street and pretended to die (die-ins) as a strategy to disrupt business-as-usual.[47] Squatter Punks in San Francisco had already opened the "Vats" in 1983, also known as the "Punk Hotel," a place for visiting bands and after-concert parties. "The Punk squatting was an inspiration for other anonymous squatter groups to feel a sense of cohesion in an everyday type of radicalized politics of land, ownership and the production of space in an urban environment."[48] Other squats opened and were quickly closed by the police. By the end of 1984 , a Rock against Rent concert was held to gain support for squatting. Their efforts however, did not maintain the squatting momentum in San Francisco. As the 80's moved on, Punks, anarchists and pacifists formed national alliances to organize protests and a sensibility that still exists among Punk girls.

I: What was New York squatting like?
Theresa: Where my squat was in NY, everyone spoke Spanish so we didn't really hang out with people who lived right next to us but most of the time people didn't really talk to us because they think that something weird is going on inside your building so they don't socialize with you. I'm not sure, I've never talked to any neighbors of the squat. Like on 9th Street there is a squat and next door there is a big crack building so you're not going to be hanging out with them.
I: How did you become a member of your squat?
Theresa: They vote you in like if you are a junkie or thief they are not going to like want you there.
I: What kind of people are there?

Theresa: In the squat I was living in for a while it was mostly like Grunge Punks.
I: What does that mean?
Theresa: Like, dirty squatter people like I don't know, like kind of like Punk people. There were a couple of older people who had been squatting in NY for a while they were into the newspapers and stuff there like the squatter newspapers.

The paradox for the girls is that they do not have a choice of surviving on the streets without boys, and yet, they are often dependent on the survival knowledge of other girls. Doherty was 15 when she joined the street scene. At the time of the interview she was 17. Though she rejected all sexuality categories, she was having sex with another woman at the time of the interview. Her interview exposed typical gender discourse among young women living in squats. Generally, it was only after young women moved away from squats, or while remembering past situations that the sexism of men they shared squats with surfaced in their interviews.

Doherty: I know couple of guys who are sexist towards girls but not homophobic. I'm kind of sexist. I don't know if I'm seriously sexist but I give guys a lot of shit. I don't hate men or anything. They deserve to be bitched at by me at least once per day. (laugh) They do man, they're pigs. They sit around they're slobs, they don't care. The only thing they ever do is buy beer which is a good thing and they better keep on doing that if they want a place to stay.

SUMMARY

The social production of space framework offers a broad array of consequences of institutionalized age, gender, sexual orientation, class, race and gender-identity. In the past, studies of the environmental experiences of girls were embedded in comparisons with boys' environmental experiences, or homeless adults. The history of European colonialism, housing activism, hippies and Punks informs our understanding of young women and squatting. While gender-based moralistic ideology of the last century is socially and physically evident in the development of cities; youth cultures, their ideologies and the development of environments of resistance has rarely been given acknowledged in the social history of cities.

The girls in this study have a variety of unique experiences related to many different power relationships, not solely their experiences with boys or gender-identity. The environmental experiences of young women in subcultures has been particularly ignored. Within Punk culture described by the young women in this study, there is ideology, social organization, and direction to their lives. There exists subcultural knowledge about surviving outside of mainstream society. Punks both challenge and recapitulate social norms. How and why certain norms are or are not challenged is dynamic and appears to be based on survival issues.

Young women on their own in San Francisco live in a myriad of places and circumstances that are constantly negotiated in an effort to resist dominant age, gender, race, class and heterosexual norms. They fight for property rights, civil rights and against the debasing social services that claim control and authority over their lives. They are faced with an absence of housing (never planned or intended by the government) and few employers who will accept the way they look. The neighborhoods where young women stay have dissident and transient social and geographic histories. Student activists, housing activists, European Punks, and gays and lesbians activists laid the ideological foundations for current anti-establishment youth subcultures and their landscapes. Urban development strategies and affordable housing plans generally ignore the needs of poor adults, and never consider the housing needs of poor youth. The spatial and social dynamics of homeless adults and youth on the street as well as the circumstances which explain youth-at-risk, runaways, and homeless youth do not adequately explain the reasons for homelessness, or why youth and adult homeless people stay in certain areas. The underground mythology about buildings and neighborhoods is important cultural knowledge. This mythology offers information about safety, architecture, neighborhood histories and tenancy.

Notes

[1]   Wolfe, M. & Manzo, L. C. (1990). *The social production of built forms, environmental settings and person/ environment relationships.* Presented at the 11th Conference of International Association for the Study of People and Their Surroundings. Ankara: Turkey

[2]   Wolfe & Manzo, (1990), p.8

[3]   Di Prima, Diane. (1988)

[4]   Spain, D. (1992). *Gendered spaces.* Chaple Hill and London: Univeristy of North Carolina Press. p.17

[5]   Spain, 1991, p.16

[6]   ------- (1989).*Writing against the silences: Female adolescent development in the novels of Willa Cather.* Studies in the Novel, 2(1), p.60-72.

[7]   Wright, Gwendolyn. (1983). *Building the dream.* Cambridge: MIT Press. p.22

[8]   Wright, (1980), p.24

[9]   Goffman, E. (1967). *Interaction ritual.* New York: Pantheon Books.

[10]   Thorne,B. & Kramarae, C., Henley, N. (Eds.) . (1983). *Language, gender and society.* Rowley, MA: Newbury House.

[11]   Ardener, 1981

[12]   Rosaldo,Michelle, & Lamphere, Louise, (1974). *Women culture and society.* CA: Standford University Press.

[13]   cited in Spain, 1992, p. 26

[14]   Katz, Cindi. (1993). "Growing girls/closing circles: Limits on the spaces of knowing in rural Sudan and US cities" in Katz and Monk (Eds.). *Full cirlces.* London: Routledge.

[15]   Piche, Denise. (1988) "Interacting with the Urban Environment: Two case studies of womens' and female adolescents' leisure activities" in *Life spaces, gender household employment* . Vancouver: University of British Columbia Press. pp. 159-186.

[16]   Spain, 1992, p.35

[17]   Weisberg, D. K.(1985). *Children of the night.* Massachusetts,Toronto: Lexington Books.

[18]   Godfrey, B. (1988). *Neighbood in transition: The making of San Francisco's ethnic, nonconformist communities.* Berkeley: University of California Press.; Golthorpe, Jeffrey. (1992). "Intoxicated Culture: Punk Symbolism and Punk Protest" in *Socialist Reveiw:* . Berkeley California. pp. 35-64.

[19]   Golthorpe, 1992

[20]   Heskin, 1988; Welch, Mary Beth. (1992). "Homeless But Not Helpless" in *Homelessness a national perspective,* (Eds.). Robertson and Greenblatt. New York: Plenum Press.pp. 323-336.

[21]   Heskin, 1988, p.24

[22]   Robertson, M. (1989). "Homeless youth: An overview of recent literature" Monograph of the *Alcohol Research Group,* Berkeley: California.; Robertson, Marjorie & Greenblatt, M. (Eds.). (1992). *Homelessness A National Perspective.* New York and London: Plenum Press.

[23]   Ruddick, Susan, (1988). "Debunking the dream machine: The case of street kids in Hollywood, CA." *Children's Environment Quarterly* , 5 (1), 8-16.

[24]   Ruddick, S. (1996) *Young and homeless in Hollywood: Mapping social identities..* New York and London. Routledge.

[25]   Godfrey, 1988, p.184

[26]   Godfrey, 1988 p.189

[27]   Godfrey, 1988, p. 178

[28]   Godfrey, 1988

[29]   Department of City Planning, San Francisco South of Market District Report

[30]   Coalition on Homelessness, 1993

[31]   Department of City Planning, San Francisco South of Market District Report. 1990, p. 11.10.8

[32]   Department of City Planning, San Francisco South of Market District Report. 1990.

[33]   Department of City Planning, San Francisco South of Market District Report. 1990. p. 27

[34]   Klein, S. (1991). *Imagine me, falling in love....and with a machine: The automated office and social control.* unpublished doctoral dissertation, Graduate School and University Center, New York.

[35]   Klien, 1991, p. 21

[36]   Barthes, R. (1973). *Mythologies.* New York: Hill and Wang.

[37]   McRobbie, A. (1986). "Settling accounts with subcultures: A feminist critique" 1980. In (Eds.),*From subcultural to cultural studies.*

[38]   Hebdige, D. (1979). *Subculture: The meaning of style.* London: Routledge

[39]   Hebdige, 1979, p. 25

[40]   Hebdige, 1979, p. 26

[41]   Taylor & Wall, 1979, cited in Hebdige

[42]   Hebdige, 1979, p. 66

[43]   Golthorpe, 1992

[44]   Golthorpe, 1992, p. 35.

[45]   Golthorpe, 1992, p.38

[46]   Rock against Sexism, 1984

[47]   Golthorpe, 1992

[48]   Golthorpe, 1992, p. 39

IV

Environmental Photography: Relating Places to People to Researchers

"Knowing is a striving for certainty and categorization where the categorization process is totally controlled by the observee, from the perspective of the actor, not the observer."[1]

Typically, social science uses photography to visually document already established social and personal categories, imposing these categories on photographic "subjects." Categorization maintains social order and promotes the ideas of those in authority.[2] For example, during the Depression and Red Scare respectively, pictures of poor people and those suspected of anti-patriotism produced the "gaze of surveillance."[3] The camera itself does not have power, but is imbued with power by the state's production of highly coded images. Viewed through the proper lens, the photographic subject becomes a threat to national security justifying government repression.

The study of the social production of representation, which deconstructs photographic data generated in the name of science and truth, demonstrates the lack of democratic processes in selecting the image, and the misrepresentation or over-typification of one image to symbolize a larger idea. In this way, the "photo" is used to impose control and order in a state-defined-history which supports hegemony.

Studies of photography in the social sciences reveal five visual recording categories: visual records of groups and societies, visual records of human movements, visual records of social interaction, visual records from the actor's point of view and observation involving the interaction of persons and camera. [4]

Ziller's work on the theory of self proposes an alternative model. He posits that the self is involved in every aspect of human behavior, processing of information, and emotion. The self functions as a control, mediating the environment and behavior and all efforts to understand human behavior must first attempt to understand the self in interaction with the person's environment.[5] Therefore, Ziller believes that self-photography can lead to more meaningful data particularly when people use words to describe themselves or their environments.

METHOD

It was my intention to use self-photography to bring texture and visual data to the words the young women used to describe their experiences. I discovered however, that the photos were difficult to interpret and that the process of giving the young women film and discussing the photos was more complex than I initially imagined. I told them at the beginning of their initial interviews that if they were interested in photographing their environments, including places where they hang-out, eat, party, sleep, they could participate or they could participate in only the interview. I distributed a total of 20 cameras (auto-focus, 35 mm with flash) and 450 film shots resulting in 40 pictures. I arranged to meet those who participated one week after they received the camera and exchanged more film for film they had shot. This arrangement gave us the opportunity to talk and discuss the week, including the process of photographing and any problems they had with the camera and/or the notebook. I gave each young woman a small notebook to document the pictures she took, feelings, thoughts, a type of diary to reflect on the pictures. That was an unsuccessful strategy. I don't know what they did with the notebook, but it wasn't used for the purposes intended. This made discussing the photographs difficult. There were only a few times that I was able to show the developed photographs to the young women and discuss the content and process of taking the pictures. When the young women resisted discussing the photos but instead talked about the camera getting "lost", "broken" or "borrowed" I began to question them about their experience of having a camera. Often cameras would break as the young women climbed a fire escape to the roof and lowered themselves into the top floor window, or skirted under a door held up by another squatter. Eight of the young women were given cameras more than once and one young woman who was not interviewed was also given a camera with film.

I photographed the places where I met the young women as well as places in other parts of the city where girls stay, such as the Haight Ashbury area, the Polk Street and Nordstrom coffee shop. The quasi-public and public environments took on a new meaning to me while I was photographing. I often felt like an intruder, entering both invisible and visible rooms, and landscapes. Photographing places where homeless young women stay has nothing to do with documenting a competent representation of their environment. In retrospect, I would not do that again, because I produced meaningless images, decontextualized from their experience.

I went on a photographic tour of all the squats one of the participants had used in the 4 years she had been homeless. I photographed the buildings and places while she spoke into a tape recorder describing her experience. These 11 different places and the information I could gather from discussing the sites as we toured was the most successful photographic experience because it created an immediate understanding between us that was not achieved through the other activities. The meaning of windows, walls, symbols, public art and each building became more visible as the framework for the social production of their landscapes became grounded in her experiences.

PHOTO ANALYSIS

The limitations of this type of analysis are embedded in personal and social memory, and the coercive relationship between researched and researcher documented in critical anthropology and sociology literature. My interpretations, as well as my categorizations of their photos, are based on the verbatim interviews with the young women, not necessarily while they were looking at the photos they took. Interactions over a period of time, as well as my a priori assumptions that race, class, gender-identity, and sexuality mediate environmental and social experiences, informed my understanding. The themes provided the opportunity to discuss related issues that emerged both from the photographs and the interviews.

Ziller assumes that the camera has power and that the observer can misuse that power both by choosing the pictures taken and by interpreting the photographs. However, when the camera is used directly by the actors, Ziller claims that these pictures provide insider understanding, a theoretically closer and true knowledge of the actor. Ziller's analysis however, is limited because it does not take into consideration the social value and use of the camera itself. The camera has both exchange value in the street market and cultural value since photography is an art form. Recognizing these values and their relationships to the images produced by the young women led me to an ethnomethodological analysis of the photography project. Ethnomethodology advocates the close investigation of actual courses of social action rather than producing rule-like characterizations of individuals or cultures within outsider defined categories. Ethnomethodological methods for visual analysis provided the framework to make sense of the photos taken in the context of the young women's everyday experience.[6]

Content analysis is viewed as an "objective" method used for photographic analysis.[7] It theoretically offers a systematic and quantitative approach to categorize photographic material. Thus, supposedly, if two coders were to look at the pictures taken by the young women in this project, they would obtain the identical results from the body of information. This theory, however, does not consider that the interview text, the experience of knowing the young women and the process of entering the corridors of their environments are integral to reproducing the photographic analysis. I employed some elements of content analysis, recognizing its limitations. I did not propose pre-established categories but allowed them to come forth during the interviews. While I did count photos within categories, no one category was given any more importance than another. My assumption was grounded in the belief that girls had particular environmental experiences as a result of being on their own. I did not know prior to meeting the young women that squatting was the main type of housing or that the subcultural identity would influence their environmental choices and spatial organization. I expanded traditional content analysis by using it to compare and contrast the *descriptions* of the experiences. The subcultural meaning of the photos are not immediately readable to an outsider by viewing the photos alone. The language and meaning of the pictures only became evident through the girls' descriptions. For example, pictures of metal garage doors did not express the complexity of the experience of entering or exiting an abandoned building.

There are many advantages to using a camera for gathering information with people who do not have a common language. The main advantage of using cameras in this study was to give the young women something they could trade. The camera became a tool that allowed them to communicate in a medium they respected (artistic tools), to be creative and expressive. It gave us a reason to meet again and it was used as a symbol and new identity (temporarily a photographer) thereby offering another type of cultural currency to their use of abandoned buildings. The elevated social value placed on their squatting created a commodity for the young women to trade with. There are many examples within the interviews indicating that the abandoned buildings or squats were re-established as a commodity in their social relationships with other homeless people, in political housing movements, and in negotiations with owners of abandoned buildings. The value of the squat is linked to their rights of first entry and resistance to the hegemony of homeless adults who impose rules in the squats (known as squatter nazis), thereby disregarding the rules already established by the youth. The line between property ownership and inhabiting a building was often a point of resistance used in negotiations between squatters and building owners as well as a strategy for longer tenancy and community acceptance and support. The squat was in many cases more than a roof over their head. It was a symbol of their anarchist ideology, challenging the rights of ownership and a commodity they used with other subcultures in certain circumstances. The photography project was another circumstance in which they could use the squat as a commodity in exchange for their own use, to sell or trade in.

While most of the participants did not comment directly on the photos taken, each participant did discuss in detail her environmental experiences of being on her own. Themes emerged from my analysis of the photos and, after combing through the interviews, their voices created a strained but collective image of the spatial experiences of living on your own as a girl. The resistant space they carved out in deteriorated buildings and urban landscapes was a hardship and a home that provided safety and freedom simultaneously with danger and deprivation. The complexity of constant trade-offs and negotiations within the spaces they use defies a dichotomous or cause/effect understanding of the consequences of their experiences. This chapter clearly illustrates that the dialectic expressed by girls who squat and consider themselves Punks must be explored further (with other girls as well) because the meaning of their environmental experiences is expressed in a complexity often omitted by researchers and those who use photography to gaze into the meaning of homelessness (see for e. g. Shooting Back Exhibit, 1991).

THEMES

Eight themes emerged from the photographs taken by the participants: 1) entrance and exit 2) interior spaces, symbols and design; 3) furniture; 4) one person; 5) groups; 6) public places; 7) views of the outside from the inside and; 8) art. The number of pictures in each area varied considerably and the reasons for that became evident as the girls revealed their experiences.

Entrance/Exit

Photographs of entrances and exits to squats accounted for 1% of the photographs taken by the young women. Squatting is criminalized and often observed by the authorities. Young women are often forced to rush through as they enter and exit a squat. Taking pictures of entrances and exits becomes a dangerous photo experience and one which is rarely represented by a door. Text which accompanied this theme included Lashawna's. She had not been in San Francisco for very long. She described how she entered a squat in Hollywood where she stayed for almost a week:

> We squatted one night in this big abandoned apartment building. They were trying to put it up for lease and wasn't finished. We hopped over this fence, went all the way round this yard to the parking lot and went to the side of it and climbed up these bars and went through the window and jumped down which was a long jump and it was really dark and we had candles.

The dangers and complications of entering a squat were echoed by all of the young women. Finding a squat or "squat hunting" is usually a group effort precipitated by the closing of one or more of the squats by the police. A street that people don't usually walk on is a prime location for a squat. Finding any type of abandoned building is the next step. If you don't need to sleep in it that night you can put a lock on the door to see if anyone else is using the building. Negotiating an agreement with the owner can sometimes be accomplished and lessens the dangers involved with entering. Lashawna recalled her long term squat experience:

> I have a squat on 7th and Nato Street, and that's the only place I call home. I don't tell my family I'm coming back home. I tell them I'll be back for a little while. The squat has 8 apartments in it. We actually

counseled with the manager and she has given us
permission to be there. Some of the neighbors give us
money in the morning for breakfast and that's really
nice to have that kind of support cause a lot of us
don't get that.

Few land-owners are willing to allow squatters to stay,
even if the building remains empty. Locating a squat has
become more difficult as neighborhoods which usually house
transient communities are destroyed by government neglect and
developed by corporate businesses. Punk girls prefer squats on
quieter streets, not located directly in the middle of the street
economy of the busy Tenderloin. The buildings must be out of
their day-time hang-out area but not too far because
transportation can become a problem. Claiming a squat often
requires diligence. Tia entered an old school building in the
Castro, a neighborhood with few abandoned buildings:

We broke the window, but the first time we just went
through the front door, then the door was boarded up,
so we went in through the side door and the third
time we tried to get in from the roof but it didn't
work. Sometimes its hard to get in and you have to be
pretty persistent.

Many of the squatter buildings are earthquake-damaged
and others have been abandoned due to asbestos or fleeing
manufacturers. These buildings are being demolished and as a
result, the squatting possibilities have significantly decreased
in the past three years. Empty lots or parking lots have
replaced existing squats. Dana describes how she entered one of
these buildings that used to stand on the lot:

There was a door that went from here to here and if
you fell off the door you fell in the swamp and there
were mosquitoes and nasty weird things so you didn't
want to do that, so you went across that and you went
down and it was dark, it was really pitch black dark.
I went in and went up to their bedroom and all these

people were coming in, like 50 people up there at one time.

Another time, Dana and Sue went looking for a squat:

Sue and I hated looking for squats, one time she almost died and was hanging out of this window by her finger tips dangling way up there.

Despair took part in cleaning up a squat but ended up sleeping on the roof:

There was this big metal garage door and it was chained down but there was six inches and you had to shimmy your way under it and then you had to be sure you didn't get cut by all the broken glass while you're doing that and then you go up three flights of stairs and make sure you didn't find the broken stairs and then you go up there and there is this room with carpeting and bugs.

Another building was good for sleeping on the roof:

In the alley way, we had a hole in the wall with a board covering it and when you go through that hole you go up the stairs to the roof which was OK once you got up there.

Amber discusses the perils of being seen by outsiders:

It was really difficult because you had to climb up on the roof to get in and then climb back down to get into the squat really quickly. One of the people across the street saw us crawling in and out and one of them called the cops and we had to leave really quickly. A couple of us had to jump down and it's three stories high so we had to hang by this ledge.

Robin's squat tour emphasized the difficulty of getting in and out of squats.

> We got into it by climbing up the roof, hopped between two things as far as our legs would go and there would be a drop of three stories and we would jump into the squat.

Interiors

Another theme which emerged from the photographs and interviews were interior spaces of the squats. These pictures (12%) depicted the size of the spaces and the dirt and vermin that was usually swept into a neat pile, if possible. Other interior photographs (discussed later) included the themes of furniture (8%), individual people (10%) and the view to the outside from the inside (5%). These three areas were discussed at length during the interviews.

Though there were no photographs of Theresa's New York City squat, where she lived for a year and one-half. In New York, there are laws to "protect" squatters, her description is important as contrast and comparison to San Francisco squats.

> It was a 6 story building and three room apartment I shared with another woman from my hometown in upstate New York. We had electricity and furniture, rugs. Anything you want you can find on the streets in New York. We didn't have running water, we had a gas station across the street and we'd fill up water containers. I didn't shower very much, though I knew a couple of people who had showers.

Some of the young women who participated in the photography were friends or "family" and squatted in the same squats either concurrently or at different points of their homelessness. One squat in particular, now burned down, provided shelter for an unusually long period to a number of young women, due in part to the design. For example, Shannon had lived in at least 12 different squats in 3 years. The longest she lived anywhere was 6 months in this squat. She described:

> It was an old music studio, and it took 115 firefighters to put out the fire. I think the "nazis" burned it down, they had threatened. Well I lived there for 6 months. I had a secret room. You had to move a wall. You walked in through this one room and you moved this wall there would be a little hallway and you would put the wall back then walk down this tiny corridor that was very thin and a lot of bigger guys has to walk sideways and you came to a door that was three feet tall that came off and then you opened another door that came out of the hinge and you came into the room and you could stand up. The doors were only three feet tall but the rooms were normal. I guess it was an old storage space and it was really clean and warm and it would be pitch black; there were no windows. You could sleep until 5 p.m. and not know what time of day it was.

The places squatted were usually dirty and infested. Without an alternative, Punk girls would make the best of it:

> We fixed up places, we built rooms where there weren't any, we cleaned up the rubble and bird shit and scraped and scrubbed and sweat and made a little house.

Rooms were important to a well designed squat because lovers and "single best friends" usually slept in close proximity to each other. Secret rooms could hide you from police or intruders when you were too ill to leave the squat. For example, Robin was ill with bronchitis one winter. The rain was too much for her to negotiate for an entire month and she luckily found refuge in a squat:

It was a loft and it had boxes around the loft and it
looked like a shelf but it had a ladder. I could pull up
and hide it under the staircase. It was my own room.
Basically it didn't look like a room. The police would
come in and I could hide in my room and not be found. I
could stand up and not hit my head on the ceiling
because the ceiling was so high. It was an old party
favor factory.

Respect for rooms, things, people and space was often
discussed by the young women. In San Francisco, there was very
little explicit structure and rules in the squats, due in part to
the instability of squat tenants because of legal restrictions. In
other cities, like New York, squatting is more stable due to
housing laws which require a 30 day eviction notice be given to
inhabitants and a variety of other political/housing
circumstances which have created a more organized squatter
movement. In San Francisco intermittently used squats which
go through years of use and non-use due to squat busting are not
spaces which encourage respect. Amber speaks about this:

The squat is pretty dirty. It's been a squat for a long
time. I think it's an earthquake building which
means it's not safe. There is broken glass everywhere.
We tried to clean it up but it's really difficult because
some people don't respect the squat and piss
everywhere. I mean the bathtub had been used. It
was really gross. That was one of the worst squats I
had been in except for Shmeg house, I mean the name
says it all. There were so many people at Shmeg that
you didn't even notice. The squat did not have
electricity, but it was pretty warm. The squatting
scene got really bad here cause some people were
kicking other people out of the squats violently, like
beating them up. There's three or four different squats
and the people who have opened them up want to
keep them clean and safe. Unfortunately, that
creates squat nazism. If a new person comes in
unannounced they are going to get beat up and that

happens sometimes to other people's friends. It happened and it started a big war and I decided to get an apartment and work and get my own place for awhile. I have a fake ID and I can strip for a living.

In contrast to the chaos of some squats, Dana who was lovers with the "king of the squat" was able to negotiate two months of stability until her lover decided his drug was more important:

> There were 2 girls and 5 guys. I really cared about them. It was like a family and we'd get really drunk and we had stereo and someone would cook breakfast We had hot plates and stuff. Actually it was the most organized squat. We had plates and people would bring food and cook and share and would buy beer for everyone and bring drugs for everyone. It was like family. I had a lot of friends and then Olah (the boyfriend) started doing a lot more heroin. On Halloween night was the first night I came home and he had a girl in bed with him, bleach all over my clothes. He did that a lot with different girls in my bed all the time and he would be doing heroin. It was pretty stable for a while. I had a boyfriend, money, it was going the way I wanted. I wanted to do it myself, I didn't want to go to no foster home. I wanted to get a job, go to school, do it by myself. But the squat got really fucked up with drugs. You know the bathrooms that say men or women on it, this bathroom said junkies on it. This guy from New York came down to the squat and I kissed him and my boyfriend found out and jumped him and hurt him pretty bad and everyone in the squat blamed me and I was thrown out.

For many reasons girls found themselves without a squat. The chaos-imposed rules of the squat, or the power relationships of sexism and heterosexism became too much for girls to negotiate, so they tried to earn money to get an apartment or hotel room - usually with a group of people. Sometimes they would end up walking the streets all night because they had nowhere to go. Negotiating space sometimes means negotiation with homeless adults or "community organizers." Teardrop had been living in a squat for over a year when a local organization which feeds homeless people organized to take over abandoned buildings as a strategy to house people:

> ... they tried to take over our squat, they're squat nazis. They marched down with the news and broadcast people and acted like they just opened up this squat. The Punks had already opened it. I think they're really stupid because bringing down the press gets the squats busted. We don't care if they are there, but the rules they impose are not going to be there. If they keep trying to put down the rules, we will move them out of the squat. The purpose of the squat is so people have housing, shelter and they choose to do their drugs in the squat, that's the safest place to do it. Nobody can tell them different, because it's your home. We were here first. If you look at the walls you can see that punk rockers put their names up here since 1977. There are a lot of drawings. My ex-boyfriend's room has cartoons on the walls. A lot of Punks have different talents. I myself do the electricity and carpeting inside the squat. Others do the water, gas, the heating, painting. Everyone who comes in does something to improve the squat so we can stay there.

Each girl had a variety of experiences while squatting. While the hope is for stability, the lack of support from San Francisco's housing laws fosters a squat environment that is chaotic. Robin expresses the more cynical aspects of squatting:

> Basically people don't give a fuck, and we're fucked. I've stayed in so many buildings and ruined so many buildings. Those aren't even places I would consider a

squat because to me a squat is a place to make your home you know. No one cares, because we're going to get kicked out anyway, it's an abandoned building.

Furniture

Furniture was represented in 8% of the photos. Squats sometimes have furniture left by the previous squatters or tenants. The type of furniture depends on the type of building it was before it was abandoned. If there is no furniture, squatters must find what they need, carry it to the building and enter the building as unobtrusively as possible. For that reason, unless the squat is well established and stable (which means that the neighbors and police have accepted the squatters as part of their community), the squats have very little furniture. Girls frequently make do with blankets for beds or no beds at all.

Tia describes a squat:

....basically it was a 15 room mansion, about 6 different bathrooms and a basement, no electricity or water. Three of us were staying there. We all stayed in one main room with a humongous marble fire place. We used to sleep on these lazy boy chairs. It was completely furnished. I think it used to be a drug house and the people had to move out really quick cause there were all kinds of clothing. We used them to start fires. We stayed there for about a month, and one morning we woke up and people were nailing boards to the front windows and we were scared and we ran.

Other squats that were furnished had amenities which made them better squats than most. Dana describes the squat she stayed in:

We had our own bedroom. It had big murals all over the wall. I don't know what it used to be before but it was really cool. It had running water, lights, a

fridge, the toilet flushed. It had mirrors and a door
we could shut to our bedroom. We had a little table, I
don't even know where we got it and we had candles
on it. We had a mattress that we stole from this
trailer and this bookcase we turned over and put the
mattress on it like a real bed. It was so cool, it was our
room.

Another squat that was shared with adults in the old
Greyhound building and adjoining abandoned hotel offered only
dirt and a roof over her head.

There was piss and shit everywhere, floors with
dead pigeons. We would sweep away the dirt and lay
down with all our clothes on and our stuff under our
heads and it was pitch black.

People

Although I instructed the participants not to photograph
people (because they could be identified from the picture
which might become public in the future), they did it anyway.
Both individuals and groups of friends were photographed,
though in distinctly different environments. Generally, the
single shots of people were taken inside the squats, while the
group shots were taken in public places. I believe this is
representative of the spatial and social relationships within
the squat and youth culture. The girls indicated that if a squat
had many rooms people would either pair-off into couples or as
best friends. If the squat was one large room they would spread
out on the floor but generally sleep in the same configurations.
Although many people lived in a squat, each had her
individual space. Public areas were group space.

Shana explains this spatial arrangement as it relates to
sexual activity:

Usually people have their own rooms if they're in couples. I know, I share a room with my boyfriend. Everybody has their own room and only shares it with one other person, either boyfriend, girlfriend or best friend. It all works out. Just like having your own place.

Group shots represented 25% of the photos taken. All the photos are taken on the street at night and they look like any group of teenagers eating fast food, drinking beer and soda, putting their arms around each other and posing for the camera. Of course, the street they eat on and hang out on is more than just a hang-out; it is their living room of sorts, the place they make money, find needed furniture and clothing and socialize freely without the fear that they will have to run from authorities in the next minute. The public places are sometimes places to get support and converse with people outside of their "street family".

Public Places

Sixteen percent of the pictures were of public places. They include fast food restaurants, bathrooms which double as showers and plazas in front of buildings which sometimes double as a place to sleep when there is nothing else. The "rocks" (a cube-like cement fountain) at the Civic Center was also used as a bathroom and shower, and was one of the main daytime hangouts. It was sometimes used as a last resort sleeping area, often shared with adult homeless people. Hardcore pornography was also represented in the public environment shots. Lack of caring for the environment was depicted by pictures of garbage layered on a tree basin, i.e., "the young tree struggling for space." When I talked to the photographer about this picture, she said she was disgusted with the lack of caring by both the people who live in the Civic Center area and the government who do nothing to care for the area. Her discouragement came through while on a squat tour. We found many of her squats gone and replaced with empty lots:

> This empty lot used to be a three story building about three years ago. Well that's the way things happen in this city. There used to be lots of warehouses, maybe six of them and hundreds of people living in them. Now flat ground, this is the land of nothingness. I guess it's more important to worry about parking places.

Public places are sometimes the last resort for sleeping accommodations. Squats busted in the middle of the night, or other circumstances leave girls without a place to sleep. Outside living is rarely done by girls alone and will generally be for short periods of time. Doherty describes the places she slept after she returned from a trip:

> ...we were sleeping under a stairwell on the top floor of apartment building, the stairwell to the roof, in the park.

No matter how limited their options, the girls never slept alone; they were always with a friend or boyfriend. Some girls thought there were fewer non-exploitative options for girls to sleep on the street. Darlene explains:

> ...it's a scary thing for a girl to live on the streets, people don't respect girls. Anything could happen to her on the streets and especially being that vulnerable. If a guy needs a place to stay and a guy says to him, hey do you want to come stay at my place, it's straight up do you want to come stay at my place. If somebody says that to a girl, it's different, they mean they want to get laid. That's why it's scary because no one is straight up with you, they want something from you, and it's a lot harder that way.

Staying on the street wears you down quickly. The negotiation of spaces occurs in shorter intervals in more quasi-public environments, due in part to legal restrictions. The social acceptance of harassment of girls on-their-own. This is explained by Robin:

> I've slept on somebody's back porch one night. I've slept on the scaffolding by a construction site, in the alley of the youth center, in the new Greyhound station, and on this public stoop where rich business people sit and have lunch downtown. You go around the back and there is a fire escape and you get down the bottom and there is a kind of inside. The security guard woke us up at 7 a.m., At the Greyhound the security guard woke us up at 6 a.m. and we only got to sleep at 4 am. He didn't bother anyone else, just us.

Doherty had a similar experience after she was thrown out of her squat by her boyfriend:

> We had no where to stay so we stayed at the greyhound station, it was raining and freezing and it was the third night we had no where to stay. One night we spent in Carl's Jr., they let you sleep there if you don't put your feet up on the chairs. One night we were walking and walking. The wind was blowing so hard we couldn't get to sleep till 5 am and the cops woke us and fucked around with us till the youth center opened. I stayed up a lot, I stayed in this elevator a lot, I would turn it off and could get pretty good sleep until 6 or 7 am. One morning a guy opened it up with a crowbar and threatened to beat the shit out of us. Brandy was flipping out cause she was having really bad stomach pains, she thought she was having a miscarriage because she tricked a lot. Nothing was open and we were crying and I was holding her, I didn't know what to do. I begged these people to let us stay in their hall and they said we could stay on their fire escape, and it was wet and had large sewer bugs, no way were we staying there.

Despair had just moved out of her mother's house and she was living under a tree in a small town in Washington:

> I didn't have anyway of making money. I was 14 and my mom wouldn't help me get ID so I couldn't get a job. I made some money for a while sitting for my GED but after I finished that, I didn't have money so I had to move out of where I was staying and I lived under a tree. I felt scared all the time except when I got into my sleeping bag, then I was OK. I couldn't really clean up or take showers, it was impossible to stay clean. One time I slept behind a dumpster, I never thought I would do that, but I was so tired, I couldn't handle it.

Views To The Outside From The Inside

These photographs represented 5% of the pictures, due in part to the secrecy and invisibility required to sustain the squat and partly because there were few unboarded windows for light to stream in. Because the windows are central to the security of the squat, one of the few rules that squatters agree to abide by are that windows not be broken. This, however, is often more theory than practice. Dakota explains why she broke the rules:

> There were some kind of rules that were supposed to be there but they never happened and people broke all kinds of windows. I did, I broke all kinds of windows, I got really pissed off and broke the window in the bathroom and everyone could see in when you take a piss, but I was pissed because my boyfriend was strung out on heroin.

The advantages of not having any views from the inside out was longer periods of undisturbed sleep and staying in the squat during the day. This was very important especially when girls were ill and had no where to rest.

> People don't like to hang out where they are squatting unless they have a really secure squat because that's when you're going to usually get busted during the day. This one squat did not have any windows so we could sleep till 4 in the afternoon, it was rad.

Art

The representations of art (20%) are public murals (sometimes known as graffiti art) completed by artists, then tagged and overlaid with text by other artists, as if an on-going dialogue were occurring between those who passed by and those who initiated the art. The girls who photographed the artwork only discussed it when they were shown their photographs but did not discuss it in the context of their experiences of being homeless. The public art had a subcultural subtext which placed it within the ideological framework of the squatters. According to the interviews, they saw the art as another form of their squatting and details in the artwork represented feelings like anger that they could relate to.

SUMMARY

The eight themes which emerged from the interviews and photographs were: 1) ENTRANCE AND EXIT. This theme was difficult to capture in the photos due to the danger of coming and going. I chose this category because it was discussed at length by all the young women as an important aspect to their surviving; 2) INTERIOR SPACES of squats were organized according to resources available and the sociology of the specific youth subculture; 3) FURNITURE was often not available. The creativity of the young women to collect and re-use found objects made their squats more habitable and sometimes countered the horrible conditions; 4) INDIVIDUALS photographed inside the squats were not in groups, but were singles or couples, representing the spatial arrangements inside the squats; 5) GROUPS. People photographed outside the squats also represent the spatial arrangements of this environment; 6) PUBLIC PLACES represent a continuum of use. While girls rarely slept on the street public places were both safe and dangerous, a place to earn money, find food, hang-out and meet people outside their group; 7) VIEWS TO THE OUTSIDE from the inside were rarely represented in the photos, but pointed to an important aspect of their survival - windows and; 8) ART was rarely discussed in the interviews, but was photographed. The art had symbolic meaning both in the interpretation of the art and the way Punk girls interacted with it. The location of the art was also significant (usually sides of buildings) because it was viewed by the young women as another form of squatting, i.e. taking over abandoned space.

The photography gave me the opportunity to meet with the young women more than once and develop relationships mediated by the camera exchange. I initially thought I would get access to their seen world by engaging them in a photography project. Instead, the young women engaged me in an exchange of commodities beyond our own interactions. Owning cameras gave the young women an opportunity to be artistic and to trade-in their "homelessness" or squatting for temporary tools to produce images. Their environments portrayed in the photos are invisible to outsiders. Thus, using general photographic interpretation methods to gain deeper knowledge about a subculture or individual may be useless unless the discussion of the photos taken can be conducted simultaneously. The eight categories which emerged were chosen based on the interviews not the photographs. In some cases there were few photographs to support the environmental experiences discussed in the interviews. Those descriptions became as important as the photos which were taken.

Notes

[1]Weick, cited in Ziller, Robert. (1990). *Photographing the Self: Methods for Obeserving Personal Orientations.* California: Sage Publications. p. 14.

[2]Tagg, John . (1988). *The Burden of Representation.* Amherst: University of Massachusetts Press.

[3] Tagg, 1988, p.73

[4] Riis, J.A., (1890). How the other half lives:Studies among the Tenements of New York. New York : Scribner's 1939.

[5] Ziller, p. 95

[6]Ball, Michael & Gregory Smith. (1992). *Analyzing visual Data.* California and London: Sage Publications.

[7]Berelson, 1962, cited in Ball & Smith, 1992

V

The Cultural Rhetoric of Girls: A Review of Newspapers 1982-1992

"...nothing can remain immense if it can be measured...every survey brings together distant parts and therefore establishes closeness where distance ruled before. Thus the maps and navigation charts of the early stages of the modern age anticipated the technical inventions through which all earthly space has become small and close at hand. Prior to the shrinkage of space and the abolition of distance through railroads, steamships and airplanes there is the infinitely greater and more effective shrinkage which comes about through the surveying capacity of the human mind, whose use of numbers, symbols and models can condense and scale early physical distance down to the size of the human body's natural sense and understanding. Before we knew how to circle the earth, how to circumscribe the sphere of human habitation in days and hours, we had brought the globe into our living rooms."[1]

The purpose of this chapter is to discuss how mainstream newspapers represent young women who are runaway, homeless or prostitutes. I am concerned with the origin of the cultural rhetoric that informs ideas and knowledge about girls. I am specifically concerned with the power and influence of particular child and youth movements which frame the social domain of the "problems" for young women who do not live with their biological families. The borders created by adults' acceptance of these "problems," the controlling policy decisions based on this knowledge and the overall hateful and violent treatment of youth by adults are related to the production of knowledge by mainstream media institutions in this chapter.

THE SOCIAL PRODUCTION OF
NEWSPAPERS

"News is among other things the exercise of power over the interpretation of reality. "[2]

The printed media is a map of the world that we bring into our homes each day. It provides information about places and people which are outside the limits of our daily surroundings and defines a world created by the secular newspaper industry. The papers not only bring the true "world" into our homes, but reify ideas, as do maps. Newspapers navigate us through a smaller world, using selected visuals and organized information. However, there are many communities and events which are not reported in the major mainstream newspapers. We hear about other news from friends, witness it ourselves, take part in it , read it in alternative presses, and yet this news remains absent from the paper with the largest reading population and the most cultural status. Thus, bringing the news into our homes may fool our senses and mediate our experience of the full scale of the world.

Sociologists investigate the media from the perspective of social relations[3]. They posit that journalists need bureaucracies because the journalistic system of news production is itself bureaucratically organized[4]. The standard production is dependent on scheduled, reliable and predictable quantities of raw material (the facts, as defined by the establishment). The basis of the journalistic accounting system is the rationale for capitalist economy; the raw material received by the news bureaucracy is like a subsidy to the media. The values and messages created by the news industry are the center of communication research[5].

The world brought to us through the newspaper is narrow [6]. Facts do not arise out of thin air but are fashioned out of concepts and particular methods based on value judgments. Different value judgments produce different facts. So-called enduring "American" values (with their roots in religious-thinking and the progressive era) are shared by politicians and journalists and serve business interests. Enduring values advocate democracy, pay allegiance to small town pastoralism, support individualism and moderation and preach order and family values. Mainstream family values view poor and single parent households as the "bad ones" and as a result, are blind to structural faults within the system. News and social science literature share an ideological perspective in the social construction of girls. Similar to social science, the news media create methods of validating their ideas, by simultaneously gleaning data from and legitimizing the religious and corporate state. Newspapers reflect and promote images and ways of knowing poor and homeless girls based on morality, with the intent of controlling female behavior. While there are differences in the creation of institutional structures, (i.e., canons of "legitimate" abstract knowledge inculcated in schools and day-to-day facts viewed in the socially accepted newspaper), the news media generally decontextualizes the experiences of homeless, runaway girls as systematically as social science research neglects to report the complexity and contradictions of their studies.

The context of the "message" produced in relation to the receiver (readers) is central to understanding the more quantified mass communication research. The message is the narrative. The context includes the raw materials used, where the message is acquired (i.e., the relationships developed to produce the facts), and how influential the message is to the readers. One of the main areas of quantitative research is agenda setting, which assesses the relationship between message and reader and the influence of the news in inducing a greater sense of importance in a particular issue for an individual. Agenda setting is based on the theories of Lippman, an early mass communication theorist who believed that news provides the information which people need to see the world they cannot touch. [7] While most quantitative research supports this idea, (implicit in this idea is a value that producing social knowledge is good for society and democracy) studies regarding the efficacy of agenda setting find that stories about victims or personal travails are not effective. If one of the main purposes of the newspaper is to promote a collective social knowledge by setting agendas, then personal tragedy does not fall into the realm of news worthiness. [8] The domain of the problem surrounding runaway girls and homelessness is viewed as a personal tragedy instead of a systemic issue and therefore not news worthy. If girls are not news worthy, what theoretical framework is used to publish articles about girls-on-their-own?

Gusfield's study (1980) on drunk driving as a social problem explains, "The most subtle forms of social control are those we least recognize as such. Precisely because the categories of understanding and meaning provide so powerful a constraint to what we experience and how we think about that experience, they prevent awareness of alternative ways of conceiving events and processes. Because they lead us to "see" the accustomed forms as the only reality, they minimized and obscure the possible conflicts and the volatile decisions that have helped construct 'reality'. "[9]

A REVIEW OF NEWSPAPER COVERAGE: 1982-1992

In a review of five national newspapers (*Los Angeles Times-Home edition, New York Times-Late and National, Christian Science Monitor-National Edition, Wall Street Journal-East and West edition and Washington Post-Final edition*) over the ten year period from 1982-1992, under the keywords, "runaway girls", I uncovered 5 articles; "female adolescent" had no articles listed, "teenage prostitutes" had 4 articles catalogued, "runaways" had 36 articles, "street kids" had 28, "homeless youth" listed 63 articles and "youth" listed 5, 386. A sub-search under the category of "poor" listed 94 articles. Many of the articles are cross-referenced which leaves a total of 84 articles that discuss the social problem of homeless and runaway youth.

1982-1992: Total Number of Articles= 84

Newspaper Name	Number of Articles
LA Times	11
NY Times	51
Christian Science Monitor	14
Wall Street Journal	2
Washington Post	6

None of the articles were duplicated in another paper on the same day or week. Thus, the idea that homeless or runaway youth are news is a false notion. They were treated as a special feature related to local news. There was no national news related to homeless or runaway youth.

The context for 30% of all the articles was to praise the work of a youth service program or a T.V special that did exceptionally good work in discussing a "teen issue", like suicide. Ten percent of the articles were written primarily to discuss a new study, for example, the lack of educational services for homeless children or the Federal Government's plan to pass legislation impacting on homeless youth. The remaining 60% portrayed the deviant and transgressive behavior of youth as the result of abusive families.

The lack of interviews with young people themselves is difficult to accept from the perspective of journalistic rigor. Only 5% of the writers of articles actually talked to a young person. Often case studies used testimonials from service providers who "know" the youth, or ethnographic researchers' reports. Seventy percent of the case studies were about boys, approximately 30% included girls and boys. The only article which focused exclusively on girls covered a sex ring, involving adult exploitation of young women. None of the young women were interviewed for the article. In fact, none of them could be found.

Fifty percent of the articles surveyed contained photos of boys. The photos depict boys sitting on the street, staring off into space, sharing and eating food with other "homeless boys,"

Fifty percent of the articles surveyed contained photos of boys. The photos depict boys sitting on the street, staring off into space, sharing and eating food with other "homeless boys," all from a distance. One wonders if the youth in the photos are the young people the reporter is talking about and if the reporter even talked to the young people. The photos seem to be without context and at best, the visuals are ambiguous. Still, the ambiguity could be interpreted by the reader, based on the content of the article, which depicted these youth as aimless, hopeless and probably high on drugs.

The typifications of the homeless and runaway girls were almost always prefaced in tragedy; usually her suicide. In 90% of the articles, the cause of her victimization is said to be her parents (blamed or not). The following quote epitomizes the discourse, " If parents won't be parents, what can be done to close a gap in the legal system that allows teenagers to destroy themselves."[10]. Fifty percent of all articles blame the family for the runaways and describe the children as unwanted "throwaways" who are sexually and physically abused. There is never a direct quote from the young woman discussing her own experience. Newspapers present no range of reasons or explanation for the girl's situation.

Each paper was equally irresponsible in their adaptive use, not only of research methods, but psychological analysis.

> "They are growing up in an extremely abnormal environment. Many are very sad, and if they are not sad they are exceptionally aggressive. The street becomes an addiction in itself, the excitement or whatever it is. All the money in the world would not get these kids off the street." [11]

One particular article discusses the psychological make-up of a girl the reporter got to know as he passed through New York City's Grand Central Station over a two year period. The impetus for the story was her suicide and his need to explain how he could not have prevented it. He provides a psychological assessment of her: "If you reached her heart it stirred up anxiety and her way of dealing was to run away.

Young people who get overwhelmed by stress feel they're entitled to be destructive to themselves."[12] The authors' generalizations about youth are seemingly compelling given the history of rhetoric about youth and society's deeply entrenched morality about young women on their own. We, the readers, are swelling with pity both for the young woman and for the author, who was helpless in his ability to assist her. We are led directly to the only conclusion possible; this girl represents a social problem that can be resolved by better laws that would allow adults to force her into an institution.

Although there are reasons to believe it, it seems too simple to accept the explanation that young women on their own are stressed, suicidal, self-destructive, anxious and unable to make heart-felt connections. Without talking to a single woman, it is suspect that these journalists claim to offer a thorough or useful analysis.

REPORTING AS RHETORIC

The most recent comprehensive evaluation of teen content in newspapers was completed by Lyle in 1968. [13] He surveyed 24 newspapers, all American National Press Association members, and reported that "57% published either columns, pages or sections aimed at youth." The main reason editors reported printing youth articles was to develop the newspaper reading habits among youngsters (66%). Only one-third of the editors believed youth deserved coverage, while 14% believed the "youth needed a forum of their own." Lyle's study examined the content of the youth articles and found that: "30% dealt with sports activity, 29% with achievement or recognition, 20% with new experiences, and 16% with knowledge." A more recent study found that newspapers cut back on using special features between 1967 and 1979 and that "teen features was diminished more than any other type."[14] In 1967, 61% of the papers carried teen pages, 45% in 1974 and 24% in 1979. Along with the decline of coverage, young readers stopped reading papers, costing the papers 2.5 million readers daily. In the mid-1970's the newspaper industry conducted one of the first focus groups to understand the loss of young customers. Many theories developed including: the effects of dependency on television news; unsettled lifestyles; historical events like the Vietnam War; and lastly, not having the skills to read a newspaper. It was also suggested that something about the newspaper itself was unappealing to young people. Further investigation revealed that young people saw reading the newspaper as an "old people's habit." They felt the newspaper was a cold, impersonal middle-aged product that spoke for the status quo and discouraged change within society. The problem was not with these readers but rather the newspapers themselves. [15]

Tracing the history of typifications for runaway and homeless girls is integral to understanding current ideas about this population. The images which historically characterize runaways is based on some observation of only boys. Characterizations include: adventurous, delinquent, vulnerable to exploitation, and the "rebellious child rejecting the adult world's expectation."[16] Other typifications are that runaway youth run to have sex, break the law, wear unusual clothes, change their appearance, and listen to "unlistenable" music. The proposed resolution of these problems is control, using legal institutions if necessary. According to public discourse these children are deprived due to poverty or family circumstances. This discourse is framed by a century old concept of a caring upper/middle class white family working in tandem with Christian values and "individualism." An image that creates a murky world view of children is the child-victim. These children are exploited by social deviants, and in some case are themselves social deviants. Advocates who concern themselves with child-victims (starting with the Society for the Prevention of Cruelty to Children, 1876) theoretically seek to protect children and punish their perpetrators. In reality, the claims and subsequent institutional support protect larger cultural systems (i.e., legal, family, religious) which deny children and youth their human rights.

According to a study by White, images of young people in the media varies over time[17]. As wider social, economic and political circumstances change, and as young people are affected by these changes, media reportage shifts accordingly.

Images of "homeless" girls rarely appeared in the newspaper before 1900. "When there were descriptions of them, they fell into two categories: those who were essentially good but had been tempted into ways that needed to be changed and the evil ones who were beyond assistance."[18] In a review of articles on homelessness in the New York Times from 1865-1900, Manzo and Rivlin found that

> ...distinctions between worthiness and unworthiness applied to children, most of whom were orphans or from exceedingly poor families. Some street children were considered to be honest and industrious children and others were described as "living by their wits", with repeated accusations that the unworthy children were "dangerous," "street sinners," and "petty thieves." The columns were filled with ethnic prejudices and implications that the children were pretending to be in unfortunate conditions. (p. 2).

In the 1980's, Runaway Organizations reported fictionalized facts to the news based on estimates. The organizations do little to challenge either the demonizing of abusive relatives or the vagueness of definitions. A census of the population of runaways does not exist. Articles reported:

> Hundreds of thousands of adolescents are running away or being forced out of their home every year.[19]

> A Federal report reported 500,000 per year. [20]

> ...3,000 young people turned away from shelters every year due to lack of space. [21]

> ...68,000 homeless youth in any one night, Congress estimates...[22].

> ...250,000 homeless youth in anyone night, ... and 500,000- 750,000 per year, reported the Coalition for the Homeless[23].

..1.2 million runaway and so-called throwaways on the
streets each year, reported by the National Network of
Runaway and Youth Services." [24]

More than a million children runaway from home every
year, a report by the Department of Health and Human
Services. [25]

Reports are characterized by the following types of claims:
"Families drive them away to drug abuse." "The mother was a
crack addict" "Yeah I was smoking marijuana. My husband left
a note said he'd be back once a year and I had to live with it."[26]
These reports confirm that runaway children come from deviant
homes. While this line of thinking offers a vindication for the
"rebellious behavior" of leaving the sanctity of one's family,
and breaking the legal and moral codes of society, in reality
there are few options for those who are "throw aways" or
runaways.

The victim typification alludes to a "new compassion" for
the plight of youth. In fact, this "new compassion" does not
seek to prevent or assist young people who are survivors of
sexual molestation by their male family members. The "new
compassion" is not addressed legally or politically in ways
that would increase opportunities for young people on their
own. The absence of reporting on the systemic problems that
face young people on their own, their poverty, the legal
restrictions of youth renders the problems invisible. Runaway
organizations promote a view that youth on their own are
damaged "merchandise", ready to hurt others because they
have been hurt. They are violent, drug using, sexually
promiscuous, and "at-risk" for AIDS. This is not a new
compassion towards youth. The perpetrators are coded as young
people's parents but for most youth, and especially girls, the
real perpetrators are their fathers, uncles, brothers,
grandfathers and pediatricians.

In the 1980's, young people were rendered visible due to
high levels of unemployment coupled with increasing societal
fears about the safety of property and person. This fueled

media stories which selectively highlighted youth activities. Few reports presented youth outside of fear and hostility inducing stories. Youth were typified as coming from bad, abusive families.

Public discourse does not address the systematic implications of abuse because the rhetoric of abuse is embedded in the ideology of fundamentalism. At the same time that the missing children's movement was growing, the child sexual abuse movement was booming. The rhetoric developed by the missing children's movement for the supposed few youth who ran away as opposed to being abducted, focused on the exploitation of youth in abusive situations (though vague in definition) who were either killed or "sold" into the sex industry. Public knowledge about child sexual abuse became popular again in the 1980's due to cases involving child care workers who were sexually abusive or using forms of ritual abuse.

Though there was public concern for kidnapping following the 1930 Lindbergh event, the business of missing children only developed in the mid 1970's. The typification of child abduction by the press nurtured public opinion. In 1988 Federal legislation proposed to penalize those who would exploit children by trading in obscene works. This conservative backlash expanded the definition of child abuse to include women who smoke, drink or use drugs and attempted to invoke hatred towards women who would abuse their children by aborting their fetuses. At the same time, there was a rise in anti-teenage mother discourse. The moral underpinnings of the broader child protection movement conspicuously blames the mother for any familial abuse, including those who would work and leave their children with child care workers rather than stay at home. The development of rhetoric used for typification by child protection advocates obfuscates the real experiences of children in a vague and often unfounded claim of abuse outside of the family and ignores the systemic issues that prevent children from real human rights protection.

The framing of youth, and girls in particular, is a rhetorical strategy, not one based on empirical or well-investigated evidence. The current rhetoric is historically rooted in the discourse shaped during the last century. Very little has changed in public discourse of youth and girls in particular. However, the experiences of young women have changed considerably due to the influences and impact of modernization, urban production, feminism, the gay and lesbian movement, increased poverty, and emerging youth subcultures

The Punk Rock culture, a youth subculture which questioned almost everything got off the ground in the United States in the mid 1970's. The rhetoric about Punks was simplistically presented in the mainstream press as rebellion of middle-class white youth. Other cultural voices in the 1970's provided new leadership opportunities for young women but did little to change the well-worn rhetoric. The Clamshell Alliance succeeded in closing down nuclear power plants, students on campuses all over the country set up shanty-towns in front of administration offices, insisting that Universities divest in South Africa, and Womyn-land and peace camps organized by young lesbians challenged militarism and patriarchy.

It is at this moment, this heightened level of female youth participation in challenging the social order, that the missing children organizers made a radical change in focus, from the child-victim to the plight of the parents. There was no public discussion of who or under what circumstances children were missing. The missing children industry staff and volunteers, without clear empirical evidence, claimed that missing young people were abducted by deviants who would sexually molest them, turn them into drug users and sell them on the streets for sex. This in turn was printed in the mainstream (secular and religious) newspapers. With all this "public" support, the conservative government of the 1980's needed very little encouragement to support the National Center for Missing and Exploited Children in 1984. The missing children's movement and the mainstream press promoted parental empathy with images and religious rhetoric of Satanists, social deviants, and sinners, referring to stranger child abductors.[27] In reality, only a small portion of reported missing children were in fact missing as a result of abduction. Most were runaway and others still may have been part of youth movements who wanted nothing to do with adults or the social order .

The social "value" promoted by the missing children's movement is the parent as potential victim. It encourages parents, through questionable tactics and political motivation, to fingerprint and file photos of their children with the local police as a supposed measure of increased protection and possible abduction prevention. The definition of a missing child is never clear, nor do these advocates investigate or publicize the reasons why children were missing. The few runaways publicly discussed by these advocates are believed to be from abusive families. The missing children advocates promote pathologizing individuals as criminals or perverts instead of looking at the complexity of the larger social issues. These larger victim based organizations are generally the reporters source of information. Legitimizing themselves and reifying parental sympathy at the same time. All of this has the effect of obscuring the relationships, situations, environments, and systemic treatment of young women in the dominant culture.

Girls' voices are conspicuously missing from the press coverage. I can only hypothesize that if girls' stories were honestly told, if the voices of "runaways" were heard, it would complicate the existing sympathy for parents and reveal the hidden religious agenda at the root of popular ideology. The moral underpinnings of the rhetoric developed for missing children seems to be connected to the agenda of enduring family values. Reviewing the articles in the secular press and in one religiously-affiliated newspaper for the past ten years indicates that the controversy one might expect to be part of the domain of this issue is, in fact, missing.

SUMMARY

My concern in this chapter is with the theory of child protection used by reporters as the major framework for the development of public knowledge within which "runaway", "homeless" and girls on-their-own are represented in the five national newspapers over a ten year period. The nearly exclusive attention paid to stranger abductions, the child pornography industry, sexual abuse by child care workers, and ritual abusers, contrasted with alternative frameworks such as

systemic issues that face young girls on-their-own, is not yet
developed by reporters as the focus of news. The stories told by
the news are congruent with and fortified by the social
construction of girls on-their-own in the social science
literature. The agencies which serve young women are
responsible for allowing and perpetuating these one-sided
stories. Their collusion with the mainstream press accumulates
hostility towards young women by adults and by the young
women towards authorities who would allow this to happen.
The borders between adults and girls are thick with tension and
girls fear the betrayal of their voices, their side of the story.

It is apparent from my discussion that the newspaper focus
is influenced by a collective agreement about young women and
the concern for gender order and disorder. The typification of
young women as tragic, suicidal, victims of neglectful parents
and throwaways seems to be the only story told. The 84 human
interest stories I found in 10 years of national reporting
indicated a lack of "news" about the young women's' situation
from their perspective. The invisibility of their side of the
story is evidence of the morality deeply embedded in the
industry. The newspapers' stereotype is reinforced by
organizations and policy makers preventing girls who live on
their own from vindication. These stereotypes obstruct the
creation of positive resolutions to the real dilemmas they face.

The collection of news stories I found is an important source
of cultural knowledge. It brought to light the institutions
which benefit from the negative views constructed by the news
media. While sociological studies of the power of news and
opinion attribution is debated in the field, the day to day life
of young women is impacted by their sense that no one is
concerned with who they are or what they think.

Notes

[1] Arendt, Hannah. (1958). in Greenwood, David. (1964). <u>Mapping.</u> Chicago:University of Chicago Press. p.39.

[2] Gans, H. (1979). *Deciding what's news.* New York: Pantheon. p. 81.

[3] Epstein, J. E. (1973). *News from nowhere.* New York: Vintage Books; Gans, H. (1979). *Deciding what's news.* New York: Pantheon.

[4] Fishcoff, B.,

[5] Gans, 1979

[6] Gans, 1979

[7] Lippman, W. (1920) *Liberty and the news,* New York: Harcourt, Brace, and Howe.

[8] Iyengar, S. & Donal K. (1987). *News that matters.* Chicago: University of Chicago Press.

[9] Gusfield, J. (1981). *Drinking-driving and the symbolic order.* Chicago & London: University of Chicago Press. p. 28.

[10] Hevesi, D. (1988, October, 2). Running away. *New York Times Magazine,* p. 30.

[11] Hevesi, 1988, p.35

[12] Barden, J. (1990, July, 8). Runaway youth jailed, homeless group says. *New York Times,* p.12.

[13] Lyle cited in Stone, G. (1987). *Examining newspapers* . Sage Publications: California and London.p 37.

[14] Bogard, cited in Stone, 1987.

[15] Bogard, cited in Stone, 1987.

[16] Best, J. (1990). *Threatened children: Rhetoric and concern about child victims.* Chicago: University of Chicago Press. p.4

[17] White, R. (1990). *No space of their own: young people and social control in Australia.* Australia: Cambridge University Press.

[18] (Rivlin, L. & Manzo, L. (1988). *Homeless children in New York City: A view from the 19th century.* Children's Environment Quarterly, 5(1), 26-33.

[19] Reed, M. (1993, February, 20). New breed of homeless on the streets of Los Angeles. *Los Angeles Times,* p. B1.

[20]   Douglas, M. (1990, October, 31). Helping parents reclaim their children and leave drugs. *New York Times*, p. A20.

[21]   Daly, S. (1988, November, 14). New York City Street Youth. *New York Times*, p. A1.

[22]   Gross, J. (1988, December, 12). Help for street kids when nobody cares. *New York Times*, p. A16.

[23]   Cahill, B. (1989, January, 22). Children: vulnerable in California. *Los Angeles Times*, p. 3.

[24]   Jones, L. (1987, May, 19). Youngsters share plight of homeless. *Los Angeles Times*, p. 1.

[25]   Mc Bride, A. (1987, June, 9) Homeless children: a compelling need. column. *Washington Post*, p. WH6.

[26]   Hevesi, 1988

[27]   Best, 1990.

VI

Instructions For Crossing Invisible Borders

INTRODUCTION

In Kevin Lynch's *Growing up in Cities,* adolescents still living with their families were interviewed in four different countries to examine how youth use space in their neighborhoods as a way of understanding their daily life experiences.[1] The most significant finding was that young people do identify with places, and that places inform their identity and development. Young people, in a similar fashion to adults, look for representation of themselves in the world and when they can imprint themselves on a place, it is a confirmation of their existence in a world which often misrepresents and stereotypes adolescents. I thought I could use this work as my stepping stone into the investigation of young women. According to Lynch's study, researchers just walked up to the adolescents wherever they were, asked questions: their favorite and least favorite places, the places in which they rest, sleep, eat, play, and how they get from one place to the other. They readily gave the researchers the answers to their questions. The youth were also asked to draw a map of the area and indicate the places they go, and how they modify (if they do) their environments and why. According to Lynch, they did what the researchers asked them to do. So why was my research with young women so difficult?

Stereotyping adolescents, and in particular young women who live on their own, has many consequences. The long term and cumulative institutional responses by adults to youth has created a hostile relationship between young women, who understandably want to live their day-to-day lives without adults, and the tensions of authority and service providers. The strain created offers young women and women little chance for direct communication or the possibility of developing a respectful relationship. This was the focus of my work, to understand the borders between young women and women, borders which are dynamic and can change from day-to-day depending on a variety of factors. The borders generally keep adults at a safe enough distance so that the young women are not threatened. Borders between us would change depending on the level of safety and danger in the physical environment. Changes would occur when a young woman's squat was discovered and shut down, if her belongings were searched and confiscated, if her money was not stolen, if her pets were fed and safe, if her friends were safe from authorities, if she was not denied services because of the color of her hair, or the number of body piercings, nor refused needed health care because she was high. For all these reasons and more, I was kept at variable distances by all of the young women I met for the entire time of the study.

Since I intended to interview the young women, I had to address the distrust. I did not ask questions that, though they seem "natural", reflect invasive professional attitudes. Many of the participants reported to me that they never told the truth to any adults and that they said what they thought would get them what they needed. Since I was not connected to any service or social control organization I feel that my judgments were not as important to them. I used ethnomethodology, using their words and ideas to ask the questions. I was particularly aware of their frustrations with questions about sexual behavior and sexual risk taking. HIV education and prevention programs are ubiquitous in programs serving youth in San Francisco. When we did talk about sex, we discussed the spaces available, the gender and race of their sexual partner or anything else which might be a factor in the expression of their sexuality. They reported that they appreciated not having to answer questions about their safe or un-safe practices which they thought were dumb questions, because anyone living on the street is at risk for AIDS. Since I am an HIV educator, I sometimes offered latex and lubricants at the end of the interview and they often had questions about recent changes in HIV prevention information. I don't pretend to think that everything they told me was "true," but rather a mixture of fiction and non-fiction. That is all any study of personal histories in the context of institutional power inequities, poverty, violence and trauma can presume to report.

THEORETICAL FRAMEWORK

This project is based on a modified grounded theory approach to research. The major intent of the grounded theory strategy is to systematically seek the full range of variation for the phenomenon under scrutiny.[2] The modification in this study are my a priori assumptions that class, gender and sexual identity modify experiences. If this were a "true" grounded theory project, I would not make these assumptions and all categories of analysis would emerge from the study. The explanatory conditions brought into analysis are not restricted to those that seem to immediately to bear upon the phenomenon under study. I included conditions that derive from broader societal contexts such as economic conditions, social movements, trends, and cultural values. These do not function as mere background to the analysis but constitute the atmosphere in which the theory is generated. They led to an understanding of the walls of the borders between young women and women.

This approach allowed me to make necessary methodological and theoretical leaps of logic. For example, I interviewed people in a variety of places, which led to different relationship outcomes. I found that crossing borders between the young women and myself was more effective when we met in my home. There, we would cook a meal, sit and talk. Sometimes the interview occurred at their next visit. In the privacy of my home, they knew I respected them because I let them enter my home. Their guards were down, or maybe they were just being polite. In any case, generally I maintained a longer relationship with young women I could interview in my home.

There was never just one issue which came between us. It was not just age, or race, or class; it was all of these things as well as the local activity of the police the night before, or the treatment of one of the young women by a youth service provider last month, or the grief about the 15 year old young woman who fell 7 floors in her squat and was paralyzed, or the gender relationship between boys and young women. Grounded theory allowed me to pull together a omni-directional, multi-layered, non-static thinking process that was unwed to professional canons. This theoretical approach was ultimately more complex and useful than the theoretical frameworks which already exist regarding "deviant young women".

DATA RECORDING

I audio taped all interviews and tours and transcribed them verbatim. I intended to gather and analyze data as a concurrent process allowing the themes which emerged to guide the process of selecting informants and interview participants. Due to the nature of this type of research, a variety of factors shaped the sampling design.[3] Early on, I realized that my sampling technique led me not only to girls who were homeless, but specifically to Punk identified young women. I decided to focus my research on this particular youth subculture. I added questions about being a Punk and even re-interviewed participants focusing solely on their experiences as female Punks. In this way, the participants themselves defined a key analytical category.

There are a number of youth subcultures in San Francisco and many co-exist in similar geographies. Further research in the Tenderloin will uncover a variety of homeless young women who belong to groups and organizations not identified in this study. The implications of acknowledging the differences is critical to working with youth. Youth subcultures stay in different areas within urban environments. While there may be overlap among some youth subcultures, researchers who want to work with youth must know the geographies of their group, as well as the multiple factors which influence the borders surrounding the divisions between the youth and adult worlds.

Sampling popular printed images of homeless young women during the period of 1982-1992 was chosen because only those years are indexed on the library computer at the University of California at Berkeley.

DATA ANALYSIS

Data analysis occurred concurrently with data collection. This was not a linear process but one where the analysis informed the process. The underlying assumption of the analysis was that people and documents under examination are situated in historical, socio-cultural, and political, circumstances which affect young women's material reality and experiences of physical settings. A hegemonic system determines the influence of these factors on the production of space. One of the outcomes of this system is a large un-housed and marginally housed female youth population. The young women expressed anger and frustration about these decisions, and linked it directly to their decision to be Punks. Some young women explained why they needed to dress the way they do, why they needed to be loud, why the music they listened to was loud. They wanted adults to be imposed upon (not scared) by their presence and they wanted adults who share their environments to think about them while shopping from store to store.

I used narrative analysis to understand the structure of the stories, how the stories were linked to cultural and historical information, how events were conveyed, and how they are linked to time.[4] I employed coding techniques which labeled data with as many codes as apply and created a matrix which cross-classified categories that emerged. I imposed a structure of difference in the sampling, a priori deciding to interview heterosexual, bisexual and lesbian young women and comparing the differences in stories and reported sexual identity. There were many conflicting stories about the importance of sexual identity. While Punk culture has a guiding policy based in an anarchist philosophy, they have not created environments in a counter- hegemonic fashion with regard to sexual orientation. There are no safe-places for lesbian and gay youth. The contradiction between the ambiguity of the Punk rockers' sexual orientation, reported as bisexual or not complying with existing categories, and the experiences of gay and lesbian youth is a theme which consistently emerged in their complex narratives. Some of the young women were resistant to discuss these contradictions, "I don't know, I'm not gay" when pressed for some analysis of the Punk space and attitude of gay and lesbian youth. Contradictions around race were also evident from the small number of young women of color within their social networks and participants response to questions about the underlying racial biases of Punks. The denial of any racism, sexism or homophobia within their group was difficult to understand in the context of their philosophy. I presume that their world view which was nihilistic anarchism rejected all categories and therefore did not criticize themselves outside the construct they created for themselves.

CREDIBILITY & ETHICS

To address the issue of credibility as an outsider constructing an explanatory framework of a sub-culture of which I was never a part. I gave my thesis proposal to a few of the participants and to formerly young people on their own and asked them for feedback. It was important to know if they recognized, understood and accepted my interpretation of their experiences.[5] As I discussed earlier, the contradictions around race and sexual orientation were hard to get an external validity check on. This also occurred with my analysis of the gender and power relationships. The young women initially disagreed with my analysis, perhaps because they did not want to be viewed in normative gender roles.

Critical ethical issues in this research included consent forms which assured the confidentiality and safety of the participants. In the interviews, the participants were admitting to breaking the law since individuals under the age of 18 who are not under the supervision of adults can be jailed. It was therefore, essential that I protect their identity. While some participants chose to photograph the places they created. I instructed them that no pictures should contain people, identifiable street signs or addresses of squats currently being used. Generally, participants have street names as another layer of protection between them and outsiders. Although usually known by close friends, their given names are rarely used. I obtained verbal rather than written consent before each interview so the young women would not need to sign a name. The consent process consisted of giving each participant a written information sheet about the study's background, my background, purposes, procedures, and plans for dissemination of results as well as verbally instructing her that her participation in the interview indicates consent. Each young woman was told that at any time she could stop the interview process or decline to answer any question.

I felt morally and ethically responsible for creating a research situation which would guard participant safety. This meant that participants must be safe from forced disclosure, fears of reprisal and attacks on their self esteem. Participants must be met with respect, honesty, and openness to their point of view. Given the dynamic nature of this research, I negotiated research procedures as necessary, recognizing distress related to the research process. Participants who chose to discuss nonconcensual sexual experiences were clearly in distress during the interview and often cried or tried not to cry. All of the young women in this study have experienced unwanted sexual acts both with strangers and men in their biological family, and in some cases, with male Punk Rockers. In some situations I turned off the recorder and we talked until the participant wanted to continue the interview or leave. Generally a feeling of support emerged between us. For my own safety, I planned to have a research partner walk with me. This was never possible because I did not have the money to pay her. Instead, I tried to put myself in public situations during day light hours where I didn't feel threatened. That was not always possible, but I suggest that future work be conducted in the manner I had planned.

INTERVIEWING: GUIDE, LOCATION AND DURATION

I started each interview with an explanation of what I was doing and asked the participants to tell me all the places they stayed from the first time they were on-their-own. I asked participants the reasons they slept in certain places, if those places have changed over time, and whether their knowledge of the area is important to understanding why they feel OK about sleeping in some places and not others. A interview guide was eventually developed and reformulated throughout the research process, depending on contingencies of particular interview situations and emerging themes. In later stages of data gathering and data analysis, questions about building knowledge, gender relationships, and Punk culture needed further verification. Content validity of questions were substantiated continuously by checking with participants, informants, and other members of the homeless adolescent communities about their appropriateness and quality.

The interviews lasted for as long as the participants allowed. They were held in department store coffee shops near the participant's hang-out location, in cafes in other neighborhoods, in jail and in my home. Though I initially thought I would be able to spend extensive time with participants, sometimes moving through the day with them, it was impossible to develop that level of intimacy given the short amount of time I had to collect data. I did meet with them multiple times for shorter periods of time and did hear about them from other participants over the year. I would often run into them on the street and "casually" catch-up with them over the period of a few minutes, sometimes going out for coffee.

During one of my outreach/recruiting efforts I was arrested. I went to the illegal needle exchange in the Polk neighborhood. I knew many of the street workers from previous political and research work. We were standing in a dark cold alley discussing the groups' reservations about my recruiting young women who use the exchange when a police car drove up. They confiscated all the clean syringes and arrested the needle exchange workers, myself and one client. I did not recruit participants from this site because the exchange workers were concerned new users would be scared off, especially since the arrest gave the exchange a bad reputation on the street.

In comparing interview intimacy and environments, it is evident that the participants were most revealing and comfortable talking in my home over a meal or tea. While it may be unorthodox to interview study participants in the researcher's home, developing a rapport with young women who have been traumatized by at least one and generally a large number of adults and their institutions is difficult. Only with slow respectful contact can a young women begin to discuss the details of her life. Meeting in my home, a quieter, stable place, assisted in developing the relationship a researcher needs and was safer for me.

Demographic data were collected during the interviews. I initially thought that collecting these data would be helpful in the interpretation of interview data as well as in the comparison of findings to other studies about adolescent young women. I have since discovered that there are no other studies about adolescent young women with which to compare my work, yet the demographics were informative in terms of addressing larger, class, race and youth subcultural issues. Almost all the young women in my study were White; about 50% were bisexual, 1 was a lesbian and the remaining were either heterosexual or did not identify with any sexuality. I was concerned that I was not getting a cross-sectional representation, because I am White and my sample was reflecting my own racial biases. Through my commitment to anti-racist political work with a multi-racial city-wide coalition that advocates for young women and women involved in the criminal justice system, I was able to discuss this bias with coalition members. In addition, I discussed race with the young women I interviewed and I surveyed 12 youth serving organizations. I discovered that young women of color and lesbians are not being serviced by the local organizations, and are predominantly in other youth subcultural affiliations. I concluded after meeting with adults who have contacts in Latino, African American, and Asian communities that I was not going to make a dent in those communities for this study. I chose, given my time limitations, to focus on young white Punk identified women. Making inroads into an "illegal" underground population is a difficult task for any adult.

Gender relations were complex even among Punks. My ability to make contact with the young women was not impeded by those relationships. One time, at the Nordstrom coffee shop, a group of "Grungies"- physically dirty, male Punk (friends of the participant) sat down at our table during an interview. The young woman I was interviewing hardly stopped talking to acknowledge them. We only had to stop the interview for a few minutes before the young woman I was interviewing told them to leave and that she would meet up with them later. The boys left and we sat there for another 30 minutes.

Violence was a common occurrence for the young women in this study and the sexual violence upset me the most. During one of the interviews, a young women reported that she had been raped only last week. I shut off the recorder and we talked for a while. She didn't seem to need any referrals because she was talking to someone and had a place to receive medical attention. I was so angry at the boy who had raped her and assured her that, if a vigilante group were organized, I would be part of it. Another young woman reported a rape and that she was prosecuting the rapist. She was not visibly upset, she was also interviewed in a youth jail and the entire interview was not reliable because she was not open to me. Institutional environments only punctuated the borders between us, the power differences and the layers of tension.

Notes

[1]   Lynch, Kevin (1977.).*Growing up in Cities.Studies of the Spatial Environment of Adolescence.* Cambridge, MA.:MIT
[2]   Strauss, A. (1987). *Qualitative Analyis for Social Scientist.* U.C.S.F. and Tremont Research Institute: London: Cambridge University Press.
[3]   Glaser, B.G & Strauss, A.L. (1967). *The Discovery of Grounded Theory: Strategies for Qualitative Research.* Chicago: Aldine Press. ; Strauss, 1987; Strauss, A & Corbin, J (1990).*Basics of Qualitative Research: Grounded Theory Procedures and Techniques.* Newbury: Sage Publications
[4]   Mishler, Elliot. (1986). *Research Interviewing: Context and Narrative.* Cambridge: Harvard University Press.
[5]   Bloor, M.J. (1983). "Notes on member validation". In R. M. Emerson (Eds.), *Contemporary Field research: A Collection of Readings* pp156-172. Boston: Little, Brown, & Co.; Douglas, L.D. (1976). *Investigative Social Research.* Beverly Hills.CA: Sage Publications.

VII

2030: Reflecting on the End of the Millennium

"Fiction and social science are usually seen as very different approaches to representing reality. They have different persuasive rhetorics, they deal differently with evidence, and they offer different kinds of rewards to the readers. "[1]

My last chapter is situated 34 years from now, in the year 2030. My story speaks to my hope for survival. The characters Darlene and Lulu were young women on-their-own in 1993. Their story weaves together the eight theoretical issues which have emerged from my study: 1) there are a variety of youth sub-cultures which young women belong to; 2) the treatment of young women is based on moral codes which are narrow and ideologically flawed; 3)buildings and places have mythology which are important information to young women; 4) "homelessness" is a social construction; 5) photography as a method for creating representations of young women-on their-own is flawed; 6) researchers, even if they are women, are not part of the young women's culture and are in fact, viewed by young women as guilty of betrayal until proven innocent; 7) the borders which I have attempted to map are the beginnings of a new epistemological landscape and, 8) young women are really smart and talented.

And so the story begins...

It was very dark, thank god there were some small pieces of candles we found in the garbage we picked from. The candles were left over from the White Night demonstration. You remember the riot after Dan White killed Harvey Milk and Mayor Mascone. I wasn't alive then, but I remember going to the marches. They were fierce and big and I was thrilled to see all those angry gays and lesbians. In fact, one of those marches was when I kissed a girl for the first time. I'll tell you about that later.

Lulu wouldn't usually go off on these long stories when I asked her about her past. My mouth would get parched as I listened to the never ending ups and downs of running through the streets, trying to stay safe and fed and somewhat clean.

Just the night before the cops had busted a squat we were staying at and I lost my clothes and my favorite music tape as I ran down the stairs, I could barely see in the dark. I felt the hot breath of the dogs that followed behind me. Their barks were so loud in the empty cavernous floors we stayed on. It was all I could hear, and I know Teardrop -that was her street name, was calling to me but I couldn't hear her. I tried to block out the yelps and then I heard someone scream and I heard her fall and the dogs kept on barking and I knew that Lizard had fallen. I didn't know how far down, but at least the dogs were off my trail and I managed to squeeze through where the window was broken. Here's the scar from the cut I got. I didn't know where to go or where anyone else had gone but I heard the sirens coming towards me and I ran. The blood was warm on my arm but I didn't feel a thing. I went to the Emergency room. I walked the entire way and it was late and the buses had stopped running, besides I had no money. As I walked to the emergency room, these guys started following me. I wasn't scared but I didn't want to fight, but I didn't have much choice. I managed to get one of them on top of me so the others couldn't hit me and after I was pretty tired, they left me lying on the street. Can you believe this happened to me all in one night? Hey Darlene can we stop and have some dinner, I need a distraction, some Diet Pepsi at least.

Lulu and I have known each other for 30 years and been friends for 20 and she has never been able to tell me what she went through when she was on her own, not really. It seems strange now to think that she was illegal and that all that she went through happened because late 20th century authorities thought that girls on-their-own should be controlled or they would run wild in the streets. I don't really understand their objection at the time, to sexually active girls living away from their family. Thank god society isn't worried about girls being girls and boys being boys anymore or growing up to be responsible adults.   Kind of like that old Peter Pan story. I guess Peter Pan was a member of a youth subculture; One where you were kind of androgynous and wore funny clothes and flew around or was that a metaphor for being on drugs? Peter Pan's culture was sweet but he/she knew how to protect herself and her friends from hurtful adults. Lulu's group was like that too and yet she would be running from authorities, mental institutions and sometimes her friends especially after she decided to be with girls.

Darlene was Lulu's closest friend, and though they had been lovers, roommates, enemies, and friends (in that order) Darlene has never understood how Lulu survived during those "Repressive Years" (1980-2010), especially as a teenage girl on her own. It seems that at the end of the 20th century, the moralistic consensus regarding girl's behavior was founded on ideas from the earlier centuries, maybe even 2 and 3 hundred years ago, maybe even older. While there were short periods in the 20th century that seemed to be more liberal, girls never benefited from it. So the problem for Lulu was a self fulfilling code because the strict codes of gender-based behavior supported by the academic fields we used to depend on to guide society and individuals would problematize girls who did not fit into their codes.   But the codes themselves were a problematic. No girls wanted to or could behave according to them, especially Lulu. Lulu was too creative, too wise, strong and independent. She had to be, in part because she was so poor growing up and her parents had accents or maybe just her mom did.   Her mom was also strong, spiritually strong and smart and worked in a local community center at the front desk. Her dad couldn't always work, but Lulu still doesn't like to talk about him. He died on the streets around 1999, Lulu found him. They never had any money because neither of her parents finished high school and minimum wage at the end of the 20th century was not enough for people to live on. Lulu left school to work by the time she was 11 and the only money she could make was panhandling.

"Dar, I'm ready to walk Pfanny and I would love it if we could walk together down to the park, it's such a lovely night." Pfanny has been Lulus' dog for the last 30 years. Those new vitamins really work. Used to be that pets only lasted 16 years max, but that discovery in Pretoria really changed the way people feel about their animals. I remember when I was little, around 1980, my pet cat Evelyn had to be put to sleep, I nearly died from grief. Back then we could only put animals to sleep, not people. Anyway, she was so soft and smart and when I refused to go to school and eat and started cutting school, my mother had me sent to a hospital where I went to school and saw therapists. I was very confused and ran from there and met Jojo. He and I would stay in old warehouse buildings. It wasn't as bad as Lulus' experience because we didn't have dead pigeons lying all over the place and crack addicts, squat nazis and junkies after us, but there were some buildings that had their own life. I remember one building that got hot and cold in different parts of the hall. It was really weird. Another squatter told us that a ghost lived there and that a girl had been raped and killed in this building and her ghost was seeking revenge. After we heard that, we left and stayed under a tree in a park. I felt so safe under our blankets and I would dream of Evelyn every night. I never wanted to go back home and Jojo was so good to me. We met others who were on their own and they believed in the powers of mother earth because she provided for us. We stayed together like a family for at least three months, cooked together and shared food and drugs. My street sister was my best friend and often she would sleep with me and my boyfriend, I loved her so much. We were all staying in an abandoned warehouse outside of town. It had been a squat for 10 years off and on. There were stories written on the walls inside the building, telling histories of who had come and gone. It was an excellent place and all the bedrooms were already set up.

Pfanny was chasing her favorite stick that night, running around in circles just delighted to be running, running and Lulu started calling her back because she would get scared if Pfanny got too far away. I could not believe how smart Pfanny was, she understood everything Lulu said to her and would respond immediately even if she was smelling the bottom of her favorite girlfriend-dog. One time, many years ago, Pfanny did go off and started staying with a guy who used to live under the bridge. He was about 20 years older then Lulu, his name was Jeff. Now he lives in the Redone District, but during the "Repressive Years" he was forced to live outside. It was bad enough that Lulu didn't have a place to live, but she was illegal, she was under 18. This guy was an adult and yet he was called homeless. I remember adults had something they called shopping carts which was a large container with wheels. Homeless adults would put their belongings in it. There were even vigilante groups who would take their carts and destroy their belongings. People who lived inside were very mean to Jeff and other people they called homeless and this group came to be treated worse then animals by the authorities. Anyway Pfanny was living with Jeff who lived under the bridge. He was a nice guy who lost his job after his lover died of AIDS and was thrown out of his apartment. He started doing some drugs in order to cope with his situation and it got out of hand mostly because it took so much time to get drugs in the underground because drugs were illegal then, but he took care of Pfanny. Pfanny and Jeff loved each other, but according to Lulu, Pfanny found her way back to Lulu. Jeff and Lulu met and have been friends ever since.

When Lulu's father died, Jeff became a surrogate father, and though adults who were living outside and kids who were living outside rarely lived together at that time, they would often look out for each other, especially when the police were being particularly repressive. Mostly Jeff stayed with his friends and they were mostly called homeless too and were outside for similar reasons. It was different for kids, we were outside for different reasons but sometimes we were called homeless too. Lulu said she didn't much mind being called homeless when it helped her negotiate for better living conditions among adults or building managers or helped her get food or clothing or things that she needed. We laugh so hard when we think about ...the camera. She had gotten so good at being a homeless teen that she was able to be in official surveys and University research studies. Once she was even able to get a free camera all because she was called homeless.

In front of the restaurants where they used to serve what was called fast food, I got two free cameras and numerous meals. At that time, we would panhandle to get enough money to eat at these places and academics who wanted to study homeless people and us would find us there. Sometimes we got a free meal and told them stuff about our lives and sometimes we got a free meal and made-up so much stuff and they never knew the difference. After all why would a smart girl like me pass up a free meal? And that one time, I got a free camera. I guess I was supposed to photograph the places I stayed at, ate at, hung out. It seemed strange to me, but I had a camera and I could get 10 bucks for it. on the street. Next week, I told you the camera broke and you gave me another one and I got another free meal. I was only 15 then and I had a boyfriend with a bad heroin habit and I knew if I wanted to stay at the squat I had to come up with some money for his drugs. I hated drugs but everyone did them. I hated boys but everyone did them. It was part of our culture, drugs and boys and though we agreed that we were open to all types of sex, the boys were not happy when the girls did it and so we didn't or we hid it or we left.

It's ironic that I met Lulu again, 10 years after I had met her on the streets. I was walking my dog Bee and she was with Pfanny and they started playing and as I walked over to talk to the owner which was dog etiquette, I realized that it was Lulu. Some of the girls I met I stayed in contact with, but Lulu was always traveling at that time, visiting her family of young women from coast to coast. There were "tribes" all over the country, working on different political projects, underground magazines, organizing squats, developing bands, art projects, crafts, theater. I guess that's how she survived those years.

One family I stayed with for over a year was very organized because the owner of the building agreed to let us stay. It was better then leaving the building completely empty. Anyway, I did the carpeting and electricity and Soli did the water and someone else did the food that's how it worked. We would produce plays about our lives and about things that were happening politically. One night after one of the uprisings, I remember staying up all night discussing politics. We wrote some articles about it and they were published in a magazine that you couldn't buy in a store. You had to know someone to get it. I loved doing the acting. I think it was 1995, we did a street play about AIDS and how the government was doing nothing to cure it or stop it. We had Dr. Dimento, that was Chicken-head, wearing a very bloody looking white coat . A woman came to him for treatment for all these different problems, but he wouldn't help her and especially wouldn't help her get AIDS benefits. It was so fucking realistic, Toto couldn't handle how serious we were being so she came skateboarding in whenever she wanted. We were avante-garde performers, but we did it for the thrill of being seen..

I loved having so much time on my hands, but then I also was so bored so much of the time. I hated school but I wanted to learn stuff about theater production and building sets. Everyone in my family wanted to learn something so we just stole books and read them to each other. Dar., you gave me a book once, do you remember? This was before we met again, you gave me some science fiction book. I think I lost it when my grandmother died and my mother cleaned out her apartment and threw out all my stuff that I kept at her house. I liked you Darlene, even the first time I met you, but I had to give you a hard time or else you would have thought that I was a woos. It did take me 20 years to trust you and even now, I sometimes don't. Why do you put up with me? Dar, you're just like one of those people in that book you gave me. There were three women and they didn't seem like they were connected to each other as they moved through the world, but they were very connected to each other through their work and politics and their communities and through the communication of their souls which they weren't really aware of. I think that's what's going on with you. and me.

The end.

Surviving the Streets

Notes

1. Krieger, S. (1983). *The mirror dance.*   Philadelphia: Temple University Press. p. 174.

Bibliography

Adams, J. (1909, 1972). *The spirit of youth and the city streets* . Illinois: University of Illinois Press.

Alcoff, L., & Potter, E. (Eds.). (1993). *Feminist espistemologies.* London: Routledge.

Alissi, A. (1970). Delinquent sub-cultures in neighborhood settings: A social system perspective. *Journal of Research on Crime and Delinquency* , 7(1), 46-55.

Amott, T., & Matthaei, J. (1991). *Race, gender and work* . Boston: South End Press.

Andrew, C., & Milroy, M.B. (Eds.). (1988). *Life spaces gender household employment* . Vancouver: University of British Columbia Press.

Aronowitz, S. (1992). *False promises.* Durham and London: Duke University Press.

Altheide, D. (1976). *Creating reality: How television news distorts events.* Beverly Hills: Sage.

Ball, M. & Smith, G. (1992). *Analyzing visual data.* California and London: Sage Publications.

Barthes, R. (1957). *Mythologies.* New York: Hill and Wang.

Bassuk, E. (1986). *The mental health needs of homeless persons.* San Francisco & London: Jossey Bass Inc.

Bell, H. (1938). Youth tell their story. *American Council on Education, Youth Commission. Washington D.C.*

Best, J. (1990). *Threatened children: Rhetoric and concern about child victims.* Chicago: University of Chicago Press.

Bloor, M.J. (1983). Notes on member validation. In R. M. Emerson (Eds.), *Contemporary field research: A collection of readings* . (pp.156-172). Boston: Little Brown, & Co.

Brake, M. (1985). *Comparative culture: The sociology of youth culture in youth subcultures in America and Britain.* London and Boston: Routledge and Kegan Publishing Co.

Bratt, R, Hartman, C. , Myerson, A. (Eds.). (1986*). Critical perspectives on housing.* Philadelphia: Temple University Press.

Breines, W. (1992). *Young, white and miserable.* Boston: Beacon Press.

Bremner, R. H. (1974) . *Children and youth in America: A documentary history:* 1600-1973, (Vol 1-3). Massachusetts: Harvard Univerisity Press.

Brennan, T. (1980). Mapping the diversity among runaways. *Journal of Family Issues,* 1(2) , 189-209.

Buff, S. (1970). Greasers, dupers, hippies: Three reponses to the adult world. In L. Howe (Ed.), *The white majority: Between poverty and affluence.* New York: Vintage Books.

Cain, M. (Eds). (1989). *Growing up good: Policing the behavior of girls in europe*. Newbury, CA: Sage.

Campbell, A . (1984). *Girls in the gang*. Oxford: Basil Blackwell

Campbell, A. (1981). *Girl delinquents*. Oxford: Basil Blackwell

------- (1989). Writing against the silences: Female adolescent development in the novels of Willa Cather. *Studies in the Novel*, 2(1), 60-72.

Caspi, A., Lynam, D., Moffitt, T. & Silva, P. (1993). Unraveling girls' delinquency: biological, dispositional and contextual contributions to adolescent misbehavior. *Developmental Psychology*, 29(1) , 19-30.

Castells, M. (1983). *The city and the grassroots*. Berkeley, CA: University of California Press.

Chase, J. (1991). *Daughters of change: Growing up female in America* . Boston: Little Brown.

Chesney-Lind, M. (1991). Patriarchy, prisons and jails: A critical look at trends in women's incarceration. Paper presented at the *International Feminist Conference on Women, Law and Social Control: Quebec, Canada*.

Chesney-Lind, M. (1989). Girls' crime and woman's place: Toward a feminist model of female delinquency. *Crime and Delinquency*, 35(1) , 5-29.

Cohen, B. (1980). *Deviant street networks* . Massachuesetts: Lexington Books.

Combs, P. & Slovic, B. (1979). Causes of death: Biased newspaper coverage and biased judgements.*Journalism Quarterly*, 56, 837-843.

Conners, P. (1989). *Runaways: Coping at home and on the street.* New York: Rosen Publishing Group.

Coe-Kryder, J., Salamon, L. & Molnar, J. (Eds). (1990). *Homeless children and youth.* New Brunswick and London: Transaction Publishers.

Davis, M. (1990). *City of quartz.* New York: Vintage Books.

Dear, M. & Wolch, J. (1987). *Landscapes of despair.* Princeton: Princeton University Press.

Debold, E. (July, 1993). *Personal communication.*

Department of City Planning. (1990). *South of Market Plan* San Francisco: California.

Department of City Planning. (1990). *San Francisco atlas.* Office of Analysis and Information Systems. San Francisco: California.

DiBenedetto, A. (1992). Youth groups: A model for empowerment. *Networking Bulletin*, 2(3), 19-24.

Douglas, L.D. (1976). *Investigative social research* . Beverly Hills.CA: Sage Publications.

Douglas, M. (1992). *Risk and blame: Essays in cultural theory* . London: Routledge.

Douglas, M. & Wildavsky, A. (1982). *Risk and culture* . Berkeley : University of California Press.

Dryfoos, J. (1990). *Adolescents at risk* . New York: Oxford University Press.

Egerton, J. (1990). Out but not down: Lesbians' experience of housing. *Feminist Review*, 36, 75-87.

Ek, C. & Steelman, L. (1988). Becoming a runaway from the accounts of youthful runners. *Youth and Society*, 19(3) , 334-358.

Emberly, J. & Landry, D. (1989). Coverage of Greenham and Greenham as coverage. *Feminist Studies* , 15(3), 485-497.

Englander, S. (1984). Some self-reported correlates of runaway behavior in adolescent females. *Journal of Consulting and Clinical Psychology*, 52, 484-5.

Epstein, J. E. (1973). *News from nowhere*. New York: Vintage Books.

Erickson, E. (1950).

Esman, A. (1990). *Adolescence and culture*. New York: Columbia University Press.

Evans, E., Rutberg, J., Sather, C., & Turner, C. (1991). Content
    analysis of contemporary teen magazines for adolescent
    females. *Youth and Society*, 23(1), 99-113.

Feldman, S. & Glen Elliot. (1990). Progress and promise of
    research on adolescence. In Feldman, S. & Elliot, G. (Eds.).
    (1990). *At the threshold: The developing adolescent* .
    Cambridge: Harvard University Press.

Fesbach, N. & Seymour F. (1978). Toward an historical, social
    development perspective on children's rights. *Journal of
    Social Issues*, 34(2), 1-7.

Fine, M. (1990.). Who's at risk? *Journal of Urban and Cultural
    Studies*, 1(1), 155-168.

Fine, M. (1992). *Disruptive voices : The possibilities of feminist
    research*. Michigan: University of Michigan Press.

Foner, P. & Ronald L. (Eds). (1989). *Black workers: A
    documentary history from colonial times to the present*.
    Philadelphia: Temple Univeristy Press.

Friere, P. (1973). *Education for critical consciousness*. Center for
    the Study of Developmental Change: Cambridge, MA.

Gans, H. (1979). *Deciding what's news*. New York: Pantheon.

Gaines, D. (1988). *Teenage wasteland suburbias' deadend kids*.
    New York: Harper Perennial.

Gilligan, C., Rogers, A. & Tolman, D. (Eds.). (1991). *Women
    girls and psychotherapy: Reframing resistance*. New York:
    Harrington Park Press.

Ginseberg, F. & Lowenhaupt-Tsing, A. (Eds.). (1990).*Uncertain times: Negotiating gender in American culture*. Boston: Beacon Press.

Glaser, B.G. & Strauss, A. L. (1967). *The discovery of grounded theory: Strategies for qualitative research*. Chicago: Aldine Press.

Giobbe, E. (1992). Juvenile prostitution: Profile of recruitment. In A. W. Burgess (Ed.), *Child Trauma: Issues and Research*. (pp.117-130) . New York: Garland Publishing.

Giroux, H. & McLaren, P. (Eds). (1989). *Critical pedagogy, the state and cultural struggle*. Albany: State University of New York Press.

Gitlin, T. (1987). *The sixties: Years of hope, days of rage*. New York: Bantam Books.

Godfrey, B. (1988). *Neighbood in transition: The making of San Francisco's ethnic, nonconformist communities*. Berkeley: University of California Press.

Golden, S. (1992). *The women outside: Meanings and myths of homelessness*. California: University of California Press.

Golthorpe, J. (1992). Intoxicated culture: Punk symbolism and Punk protest. *Socialist Reveiw*, 2, 35-64.

Goffman, E. (1963). *Behavior in public places*. New York: The Free Press.

Goffman, E. (1967). *Interaction ritual* . New York: Pantheon Books.

Goodman, P. (1956). *Growing up absurd*. New York: Vintage Books.

Gray, E. (1993). *Unequal justice: The prosecution of child sexual abuse*. New York: Free Press:.

Gray, D. (1973). Turning out: A study of teenage prostitution. *Urban Life and Culture*, 1(4), 401-25.

Greene, M. (1993) Chronic exposure to violence and poverty: Interventions that work for youth. *Crime and Delinquency*, *39*(1), 106-124.

Greenwood, D. (1964). *Mapping*. Chicago:University of Chicago Press.

Gusfield, J. (1981). *Drinking-driving and the symbolic order*. Chicago & London: University of Chicago Press.

Hall, G. S. (1915). *Adolescence*. (Vol. 2), New York: Appelton & Co.

Hall, S. & Jefferson, J. (Eds.). (1989). *Resistance through rituals: Youth subculture in post war Britain*. Boston, London: Unwin Hyman.

Hammersley, M., & Atkinson, P. (1983). *Ethnography: principles and practice*. London: Tavistock.

Harris, M. (1988.). *Cholos Latino girls and gangs*. New York: AMS Press.

Harrison, J. (1993). Taking it to the streets. *New Age Journal*, January/February. 58-65.

Hart, R . (1979)._Children's experience of place: A developmental Study*. Irvington Press.

Harvey, D. (1985). *The urban experience*. Baltimore: Johns Hopkins University Press.

Hayden, D. (1981). *The grand domestic revolution* . Cambridge: MIT Press.

Hebdige, D. (1979). *Subculture: The meaning of style*. London: Routledge.

Herman, J. (1992). *Trauma and recovery* . California: Basic Books.

Hoch, C. & Slayton, R. (1989). *New homeless and old community and skid row hotel*. .Philadelphia: Temple University Press.

Hoggart, R. (1957). *Uses of literacy* . London: Harmondsworth, Penguin.

Hombs, M. E. (1990). *Contemporary world issues: American homelessness* . Santa Barbara California: ABC-CLIO.

Horn, M. (1989). *Before it's too late: The child guidance movement in the United States, 1922-1945*. Philadelphia: Temple University Press.

Iyengar, S. & Donal K. (1987). *News that matters*. Chicago: Univerisity of Chicago Press.

Jankowski-Sanchez, M. (1991). *Islands in the street: Gangs and American urban society.* Berkeley: University of California Press.

Jenks, C. & Peterson, P. (Eds.). (1991). *The urban underclass.* Washington D.C.: Brookings Institute.

Johnson, B. & Covello, V. (Eds.). (1987). *The social and cultural construction of risk.* Dordrecht: Reidel.

Johnson, L. (1993). *The modern girl: Girlhood and growing up.* Buckingham: Open University Press.

Katz, C . (1993). Growing girls/closing circles: Limits on the spaces of knowing in rural Sudan and U.S cities. In C. Katz & J. Monk (Eds.), *Full Cirlces.* (pp. 88-106). London: Routledge.

Kirby, A. (Eds.). (1990). *Nothing to fear .* Arizona: Arizona University Press.

Klein, S. (1991). *Imagine me, falling in love....and with a machine: The automated office and social control.* unpublished doctoral dissertation, Graduate School and University Center, New York.

Konopka, G. (1966). *The adolescent girl in conflict .* New Jersey: Prentice Hall.

Krieger, S. (1983). *The mirror dance.* Philadelphia: Temple University Press.

Kyrder-Coe, J. , Salamon, Lester & Molnar, J. (Eds.). (1991). *Homeless children and youth .* New Jersey: New Brunswick.

---- (1975). Lasswell's three functions: Toward a theory of mass communication. *Sourthern Quarterly*, 14(1), 41-52.

Lee, M. & Solomon, S. (1990). *Unreliable sources: A guide to detecting bias in news media.* New Jersey: Carol Publishing Group.

Lees, S. (1993). *Sugar and Spice: Sexuality and adolescent girls.* London: Penguin Books.

Lemert, J. (1989). *Criticizing the media* . Newbury, CA.: Sage.

Lind-Chesney, M . (1989). Girls, crime and women's place: Toward a feminst model of female delinquency. *Crime and Delinquency*, 35(1), 5-29.

Lynch, K . (1977.). *Growing up in cities: Studies of the spatial environment of adolescence.* Cambridge, MA.: MIT Press.

Martin, M. (19). *Homeless women: An historical perspective.*

Matza, D. & Sykes, G. (1961). Juvenile delinquency and subterranean valaues. *American Sociological Reveiw.* p.26.

McLuhan, M. (1964). *Understanding media* . London: Routledge & Kegan Paul.

McRobbie, A. (1986). Settling accounts with subcultures: A feminist critique, 1980. In (Eds.), *From subcultural to cultural studies.* (pp.).

McRobbie, A . (1989). *Feminism and youth culture* . Boston: Unwin Hyman.

Mehrabian, A. (1981). *Silent messages: Implicit communication of emotions and attitudes* (2nd edition). Belmont: CA.: Wadsworth.

Meredith, I. (1903). *A girl among the anarchists*. Nebraska: University of Nebraska Press.

Meyerwitz, J. (1985). *No sense of place*. New York: Oxford University Press.

Miller, A., Eggerston-Tacon, C. & Quigg, B. (1990). Patterns of runaway behavior within a larger systems context: The road to empowerment . *Adolescence,* 25(98), 271-289.

Miller, H. (1991). *On the fringe: The dispossessed in America* . Massachusetts: Lexington Books.

Miller, T. (1991). *The hippies and american values* . Knoxville: University of Tennessee Press.

Mishler, E. (1986). *Research interviewing: Context and narrative* . Cambridge: Harvard University Press.

Moore, J . (1991). *Going down to the barrio: Homeboys and homegirls in change.* Temple University Press: Philadelphia.

Musgrove, F. (1964.). *Youth and social order*. Bloomington, IN.: Indiana University Press.

Nathanson, C. (1991). *Dangerous passage: The social control of sexuality in women's adolescence.* Philadelphia: Temple University Press.

Nava, M. (1992). *Changing cultures: feminism, youth and consumerism* . California: Sage Publications.

Newman, F. & Caplan, P. (1982). Juvenile female prostitution as gender consistent response to early deprivation. *International Journal of Women's Studies*, 5(2), 128-137.

Newman, P. (1973). Social settings and their signficance for adolescent development. *Adolescence*, 11(43), 405-417.

Noblit, G. (1976). The adolescent experience and delinquency. *Youth and Society*, 8 (1), 27-43.

Palenski, J. & Launer, H. (1987). The process of running way: A redefinition. *Adolescence*, 21(86), 347-362.

Piche, D. (1988). *Life spaces, gender and household employment.* Vancouver: University of British Columbia Press.

Pierce, K. (1990). A feminist theoretical perspective on the socialization of teenage girls through Seventeen Magazine. *Sex Role: a Journal of Research*, 23(9-10), 49-57.

Powers-Levine, J. & Jaklitsch, B. (1989). *Understanding survivors of abuse, stories of homeless and runaway adolescents.* Mass: Lexington Books.

Powers-Levine, J. & Hamilton, S. (1987). Failed expectation: working class girls transition from school to work. *Youth and Society*, 22 (2), 241-250.

Rapoport, A. (1982). *The Meaning of the Built Environment* . Tucson: University of Arizona Press.

Reeves, M. (1929). *Training school for delinquent girls* . New
    York: Russell Sage Foundation.

Rivlin, L. (1986). A new Look at homeless. *Social Policy,*
    Spring, 3-10.

Rivlin, L. (1990). Pathways into homelessness. Paper prepared
    for Public Interest mini-conference on *Homeless women,* New
    York: City University of New York Graduate Center.

Rivlin, L. & Manzo, L. (1988).Homeless children in New York
    City: A view from the 19th century. *Children's Environment
    Quarterly,* 5(1), 26-33.

Rivlin, L. & Wolfe, M. (1985). *Institutional settings in
    children's lives* . New York: John Wiley & Sons.

Robers, R. (1988). *The invisible homeless.* New York: Insight
    Books.

Roberts, E. (1984). *A woman's place: An oral history of working
    class women 1890-1940.* New York: Blackwell.

Roberts, N. (1993). *Whores in history.* California: Grafton
    Press.

Robertson, M. (1989). Homeless youth: An overview of recent
    literature. *Monograph of the Alcohol Research Group,*
    Berkeley: California.

Robertson, M. & Greenblatt, M. (Eds.). (1992). *Homelessness: A
    national perspective.* New York and London: Plenum Press .

Platt, A.M. (1977). *The childsavers: The invention of delinquency.* Chicago: Chicago University Press.

Ruddick, S. (1988) . Debunking the dream machine: The case of street kids in Hollywood, CA. *Children's Environment Quarterly* , 5 (1), 8-16.

Russell, B. (1991). *Silent Sisters* . New York: Hemisphere Publishers.

Said, E. (1978). *Orientalism* . London: Penguin Books.

Schultz, D. (1991). *Risk, resiliency and resistance: Current research on adolescent girls.* New York: National Council for Research on Women.

Seng, M. (1989). Child sexual abuse and adolescent prostitution: A comparative analysis. *Adolescence,* 24 (95) , 665-675.

Shacklady Smith, L. (1976). Sexist assumptions and female delinquency. In Smart & Smart (Eds.), *Women Sexuality and Social Control* (pp.74-87).

Shane, P. (1989). Changing pattern among homeless and runaway youth . *American Orthopsychiatric Association,* 59 (2), 208-215.

Sharlin, S. & Mor-Barak, M. (1992). Runaway girls in distress: Motivation, background and personality . *Adolescence,* 27 (106), 387-405.

Sharpe, S. (1976). *Just like a girl: How girls learn to be women* . New York: Penguin Books.

Shecter, S. (1982). *Women and male violence: The visions and struggles of the battered women's movement.* Boston: South End Press.

Silbert, M. (1980). Sexual assault of prostitutes: Phase one. *National Institute of Mental Health, National Center for the Prevention and Control of Rape.* Washington, D.C.

Silbert, M. & Pines, A . (1982). Entrance into prostitution . *Youth and Society*, 13 (4), 471-499.

Simons, R. & Whitbeck, L. (1991). Sexual abuse as a precursor to prostitution and victimization among adolescent and adult homeless women. *Journal of Family Issues*, 12 3, 361-379.

Skogan, W. (1990). *Disorder and declilne: Crime and the spiral of decay in american neighborhoods.* Berkeley and Los Angeles: University of California Press.

Smart, C. & Smart, B. (Eds.). (1976). *Women, sexuality and social control* . London: Rutledge & Kegan Paul.

Spain, D. (1992). *Gendered Spaces.* Chaple Hill and London: Univeristy of North Carolina Press.

Spivak, G. (1990). Explanation and culture: Marginalia. In R. Ferguson, M. Gever, T. Minh-ha & C. West (Eds.), *Out there: Marginalization and contemporary cultures.* (pp. 377-396) . Cambridge MA.: MIT Press.

Spradley, J. P. (1980). *Participant observation.* New York: Hold, Rinehart &Winston.

Soja, E. (1989). *Postmodern geographies* . London: Verso Press.

Stone, G. (1987). *Examining newspapers.* Sage Publications: California and London.

Strauss, A. (1987). *Qualitative analyis for social scientist.* London: Cambridge University Press.

Strauss, A. & Corbin, J . (1990) . *Basics of qualitative research: Grounded theory procedures and techniques* . Newbury: Sage Publications

Sullivan, M. (1989). *Getting paid: Youth and work in the inner city.* New York: Cornell Press.

Tagg, J. (1988). *The burden of representation* . Amherst: University of Massachusetts Press.

Tajfel, H. (1978) . *Differentiation between social groups: Studies in the social psychology of intergroup relations.* Academic Press.

Takanishi, R. (1978). Childhood as a social issue: Historical roots of contemporary child advocacy movements. *Journal of Social Issues,* 34 (2), 8-28.

Taylor, C. (1993). *Girls, gangs, women and drugs.* East Lansing: Michigan University Press.

Tuchman, G. (1978). *Making news: A study of the construction of reality.* New York: Free Press.

Wallis, B. (Ed.). (1991). *If you lived here: The city in art, theory, and social activism* . Seattle: Bay Press.

Wathanson, C. (1991). *Dangerous passage: The social control of sexuality of womens' adolescence.* Philadelphia: Temple University Press.

Watters, J. K. & Biernacki, P. (1989). "Targeted sampling: Options for study of hidden populations". *Social Problems,* 36 (4), 416-430.

Welch, M. B. (1990). *It's ours now: Urban squatting in the United States* . Unpublished doctoral dissertation, University of California, Berkeley.

Wiebel, W. (1990). Identifying and gaining access to hidden populations. [Monograph]. *National Institute of Drug Abuse* , 98 4-11.

Weisberg, D. K . (1985). *Children of the night.* Massachusetts: Lexington Books.

Welch, M. B. (1992). Homeless but not helpless. In Robertson, M.& Greenblatt, S. (Eds.), *Homelessness a national perspective.* (pp. 323-336). New York: Plenum Press.

Whitbeck, L. & Simons, R. (1990). Life on the streets: The victimization of runaway and homeless adolesents. *In Youth and Society,* 22,(1), 108-120.

White, R. (1990). *No space of their own: young people and social control in Australia.* Australia: Cambridge University Press.

Williams-Savin, R. (1990) . *Gay and lesbian youth: Expressions of identity.* New York: Cornell University.

Wilson, E. (1991). *The sphinx in the city: urban life, the control of disorder, and women.* Berkeley, CA: University of California Press.

Wilson, W. J. (1987). *The Truly Disadvantaged.*Chicago and London: University of Chicago Press.

Wolfe, M. (1990). Whose Culture? Whose Spaces? Whose History: Learning From Lesbian Bars. *Keynote Address at the 11th Conference of the International Association for the Study of People and Their Surroundings.* Ankara: Turkey.

Wolfe, M. & Manzo, L. C. (1990). The social production of built forms, environmental settings and person/environment relationships. *Presented at the 11th Conference of International Association for the Study of People and Their Surroundings.* Ankara: Turkey

Wright, G. (1983). *Building the Dream.* Cambridge: MIT Press.

Wurman, R. S. (1989). *Information Anxiety.* New York, Toronto, London: Bantam Books.

Wurzbacher, K., Evans, & Moore. (1991). Effects of alternative street school on youth involved in prostitution. *Journal of Adolescent Health, 12,* 549-554.

Young, A. (1990). Appeals to valueness: Objectivity, authenticity and the news discourse. *Textual Practice,* 4(1), 38-53.

Zemsky, B. (1991). Coming out against all odds: Resistance in the life of a young lesbian. In C. Gilligan, A. Rogers, & D. Tolman (Eds.), *Women, Girls & Resistance: Reframing resistance* (185-200). New York: Harrington Press.

Ziller, R. (1990). *Photographing the self: Methods for obeserving personal orientations.* California: Sage Publications.

Zinn, H. (1980). *A People's History of the United States.* New York: Harper and Row Publishers.

Newspaper References

Adrift, angry, hurt, alone: stories of 7 'throwaway' youth. (1990, February, 5). *New York Times*, p. B8.

A simple notion offers hope for street youths. (1987, September, 27). *New York Times*, p. 58.

Anderson, D. (1991, November, 10). Poor home, great rack; shelter shift could boost youth. *New York Times*, p. E18.

Barden, J. (1990, July, 8). Runaway youth jailed, homelss group says. *New York Times*, p.12.

Barron, J. (1987, September, 27). Schools are failing homeless youth. *New York Times*, p. B5.

Baum, J. (1989, Januay, 9). Youth homeless on the rise in Britain. *Christian Science Monitor*, p. 37.

Belcher, J. (1993, December, 25). Runaways: Slipping through the cracks and onto the streets. *Los Angeles Times*,

Bruner, K. (1993, August, 3). Some in Brazil see street kids as victims: others as criminals. *Christian Science Monitor*, p. 7.

Cahill, B. (1989, January, 22). Children: vulnerable in California. *Los Angeles Times*, p. 3.

Capaldi, M.(1983, February, 3). Tough advice to starry-eyed street kids. *Los Angeles Times*, p. 1.

Coles, R. (1986, November, 30). Neediets of all: children at risk. *New York Times*, p. 8.

Colker, D.(1993, March, 14). Runners spring into action for girl, family, helps teen who was homelesd during her training for Marathon. *Los Angeles Times*, p. B6.

Daly, S. (1988, November, 14). New York City Street Youth. *New York Times*, p. A1.

Daly. s. (1987, February, 3). New York's homeless children struglling to survive. *New York Times*, p. B1.

Douglas, M. (1990, October, 31). Helping parents reclalim their children and leave drugs. *New York Times*, p. A20.

Drogin, B. (1986, December, 26). Helping teen-age runaways, teams in a van... *Los Angeles Times*, p. 10.

Erlich, R. (1991, December, 10). Homeless adi too slow, study shows. *Christian Science Monitor*, p. 6.

Fineman, M. (1987, August, 8) Street kids. *Los Angeles Times*, p. 1.

Fried, J. (1988, December 20). For homeless youths, exposure to the arts. *New York Times*, p. B1.

Gaines, P. (1988, September, 29). Greyhound bus was his bed: homeless D. C. youth.*Washington Post,* p. A1.

Gardner, M. (1987, April, 7). Trying to keep my kids off the streets. *Christian Science Monitor*, p. 1.

Germain, C. (1986, December, 23). Helping Brazil street kids suvive their way. *Christian Science Monitor*, p. 1.

Glaberson, W. (1991, October, 21). Help for the homeless of New York City. *New York Times*, p. B12.

Gross, J. (1988, December, 12). Help for street kids when nobody cares. *New York Times*, p. A16.

Gross, J. (1993, April, 15). Children of the Shadows, part 6: Boys and the street: tempting Jerina. *New York Times*, p. A1.

Hechinger, F. (1987, May 5). Plight of the homeless *New York Times* p. 27.

Helmore, K. (1987, June, 30). Street children: what will become of the world's nonpeople? *Christian Science Monitor*, p. B1.

Henneberger, M. (1993, February 15). Increase in homeless youth burden shelters. *New York Times*, p. A12.

Henry, N. (1987, June 21). Aa sheter for learning; homeless children struggle to succeed. *Washington Post*, p. A1.

Hevesi, D. (1992, June, 17). Teen-ager is arrested in setting of hotel fires. *New York Times,* p. A17.

Hevesi, D. (1988, October, 2). Running away. *New York Times Magazine*, p. 30.

Horn, J. (1985, May, 3). Streetwise makers. *Los Angeles Times*, p. 1.

Hostel in Brooklyn gives homeless young men a new start. (1985, February, 4). *New York Times*, p. B3.

James, B. (1988, May, 29). Children on the street face greatest risk. *Los Angeles Times*, p. 3.

Johnson, D. (1987, May, 28). Lisa: a street girl's short bitter life. *New York Times*, p. 10.

Jones, L. (1987, May, 19). Youngsters share plight of homeless. *Los Angeles Times*, p. 1.

Judson, G. (1993, September,17). Survivors of streets put lives in print. *New York Times*, p. B5.

King, W. (1989, August, 11). On the trail of youth and AIDS. *New York Times*, p. B1.

Kotlowitz, A. (1988, September, 30). Lords of the slum: Chicago street gangs... *Wall Street Journal*, p. E1.

Krensavage, M. (1990, August, 30). Some poor kids hit the street. *Los Angeles Times*, p. D2.

Lee, F. (1991, November, 25). For gold earrings and protection, more girls take to the_street. *New York Times*, p. A1.

Long, W. (1990, July, 8). Death squads kill Brazil's street kids. *Los Angeles Times*, p. A1.

Mc Bride, A. (1987, June, 9) Homeless children: a compelling need. column. *Washington Post*, p. WH6.

McNally, K. (1988, December 26). Promise of sunshine, reality of night. *New York Times*, p. 8.

Margolis, M. (1993, July, 24). Gunmen in Brazil shoot sleeping street kids. *Los Angeles Times*, p. A4.

Mathews, J. (1984, August, 9). Street kids, Olympians. *Washington Post*, p. A1.

Micheals, J. (1992, March, 3). Report details violence to Brazil street kids. *Christian Science Monitor*, p. 4.

Navaez, A. (1987, February, 27). Youth sex ring is shut in Jersey: girls in elementary_school. *New York Times*, p. B7.

Nazario, S. (1992, January, 21). Playing house: troubled teen-agers create a fragile_family...*Wall Street Journal*, p. A1.

Perlez, J. (1987, November, 12). Thousands skip school at hotels for homeless. *New York Times*, p. 18.

Press, R. (1987, September, 11). Homegrown program helps put Sudan kids on right_road. *Christian Science Monitor*, p. 12.

Press, R. (1982, July, 19). Ways to deter and combat teen prostitution. *Christian Science Monitor*, p. 6.

Radomsky, R. (1983, January, 9). A New York school for street kids. *New York Times*, p. ED 28.

Raspberry, W. (1987, May, 4). Children of the streets. *Washington Post*, p. A15.

Reed, M. (1993, February, 20). New breed of homeless on the streets of Los Angeles. *Los Angeles Times*, p. B1.

Riding, A. (1987, May, 11). Brazil's street children: new attempt to rescue. *New York Times*, p. A6.

Ritter, B. (1983, December, 25). Rescuing homeless children. *New York Times*, p. E13.

Ross, E. (1993, March, 4). Harbinger house in Framingham, Mass offers refuse for teenage girls. *Christian Science Monitor*, p. 14.

Rule, S. (1984, January, 24). Study finds psychiatric problems in many homeless children. *New York Times*, p. 12.

Runaways fell domestic violence. (1993, March,9). *New York Times.*

Tefft, S. (1992, March, 17). Streetkids learn to hope in Thailand. *Christian Science Monitor*, p. 12.

Teltsh, K. (1991, February, 19). Shelter to protect homeless youth form AIDS. *New York Times*, p. B3.

Teltsh, K. (1987, June, 14). Priest swamped by success of job program. *New York Times*, p. 27.

Terry, S. (1987, June, 30). A world where survival is a daily battle. *Christian Science Monitor*, p. B1.

Verhovek, S. (1988, September, 19). Johny dies fleeing taunting youth gang. *New York Times*, p. B3.

Weintraub, B. (1992, July, 23). Filming Hollywood's underbely: success lures runaways. *New York Times*, p. B1, C17.

Wells, A. (1989, February, 22). Effort to reach homeless students. New York Times, p. B11.

Williams, W. (1987, March, 17). Investment sours for a Times Sq. shelter. New York Times, p. B1.

Wines, M. (1988, August, 8). Behind the park melee.... New York Times, p. B2.

Youth reported living in Los Angeles airport. (1982, December, 31). New York Times, p. A6.

Index

ageism 40
behavior
    delinquent 18, 19
    deviant 9, 11, 23
    gender correct 10
civil rights
    under 18 years old 10
class 23
criminal justice systems 10
criminalization
    lesbian 26
    race 27
    race/class 26
danger 45
Darlene and Lulu
    fiction 123
delinquency, see also
    behavior 18, 19
deviant
    female adolescents 11
deviant, see also
    behavior 9, 11, 23
education
    in 1836, 13
    vocational 14
environmental
    psychology 10, 27
Goffman, Erving 42
Hall, G. S. 19
homophobia 25, 45
Katz, Cindi 42
labor 14
    17th century, 13
    child labor laws 13
    child protection 15
    danger 48
    laws 15

organized 15
    underground 15, 48
Lees, Susan 12
lesbian
    bisexual 12, 23
    foster care 32
    punks 64
lesbian, class 25
Manzo, Lynn 39, 104
menstruation 23
methodology 112
    analysis 116
    credibility and
        ethics 117, 121
    data gathering 115
    environmental
        themes 78
    photo analysis 75
    photography 73
    research
        environments 120
    value 77
missing children 107
newspapers 25
    1982-1992, 99
    communication
        research 98, 102
    gender 100
    reporter as
        psychologist 101
    reporting fairness 27
    rhetoric 98
    sociology 97
    typification of
        child abduction 106
    typification of
        young women 103, 105

161